I0622838

The Biggest Idea Ever

Trade anxiety, fear, and burnout for peace,
purpose, and significance.

Denis Beauséjour

Former VP Advertising, Procter & Gamble

King Press

Copyright © 2024 Denis Beauséjour

Quotations are taken from various translations of the Bible:

New International Version (NIV) Copyright © 1973, 1978, 1984, 2011 by Biblica Inc., with permission of Zondervan.

New Living Translation (NLT) Copyright © 1996, 2004, 2015 by Tyndale House Foundation.

English Standard Version (ESV) Copyright © 2001 by Crossway, a publishing ministry of Good News Publishers.

The Message (MSG) Copyright © 1993, 1994, 1995, 1996, 2000, 2001, 2002 by Eugene Peterson, NavPress Publishing Group.

Quotations are used by permission. All rights reserved.

Cover design by Luke Tofilon.

Author's photograph by Mariel Beausejour Curtis.

ISBN: 979-8-9889165-1-2

Names: Beauséjour, Denis

Title: The Biggest Idea Ever - Trade anxiety, fear, and burnout for peace, purpose, and significance.

Description: A business and spirituality memoir of a Fortune 50 executive about spiritual life transformation. Access a supernatural life by faith. Experience power and peace. Wisdom from the ages, explained in the context of the marketplace. Two decades as a P&G executive and two decades as a spiritual guide to business leaders.

Subjects: Growth, spirituality, transformation, ideas, the good life, moments of reckoning, signposts, treasure, power, community, commitment, peace in chaos, generosity, family legacy, generational blessing, work with purpose, wisdom, finishing well, significance.

BISAC: BIOGRAPHY, BUSINESS, SPIRITUALITY/RELIGION

Praise for *The Biggest Idea Ever*

We learn and have awakenings in many ways, including new knowledge and information, experiences, introspection, feedback from others, and gaining wisdom from what others have experienced. As I read Denis' book, I was overwhelmed at the way in which he leads us to new awakenings through all the above. To me, the sharing of his own journey and experience was especially moving and instructive. No matter where you are, from having no interest in faith at all, to having been deeply involved in the faith journey for a long time, this book gives you many opportunities to have awakenings of your own. Awakenings about yourself, the principles and wisdom that we need to have fruitful lives, and examinations of faith and your relationship to God. I highly recommend it. Denis is not only smart, learned, accomplished, skilled and competent, but brings a refreshing vulnerability that makes learning from him like a warm conversation by the fireside. Thank you, Denis, for this gift.

Dr. Henry Cloud
Psychologist, Leadership Consultant, and
New York Times Best Selling Author

This book is utterly transparent and authentic. It is generous and humble in spirit. It seeks to share the power and wonder of believing in Jesus and realizing with joy that Jesus loves us and is present in us. Denis describes his journey through his distinguished business career and his discovery of the true purpose of life. I found Denis' spiritual insights to be rich in meaning, and communicated in a way I could feel and understand. I felt strengthened by his spiritual journey. This book will add value to your life, whether in business, marriage, family, ministry, or caring for others.

John Pepper
Retired Chairman and CEO, The Procter & Gamble Company
and Retired Chairman, The Disney Company

I've known Denis since we were in college. His journey in business and spiritual discovery is a fascinating read. Regardless of your beliefs, I think you'll find his insights to be relevant and practical. Denis' story speaks powerfully to business leaders focused on personal growth and relational effectiveness.

David Court
Senior Partner Emeritus, McKinsey & Company

We all want more of the good in our lives: better relationships, healthier families, more satisfying careers, and more meaning. Denis explains the keys to these in a clear and warm way. He provides biblical principles, applicable skills, and lessons from his own life that are easy to identify with. Denis' personal vulnerability will draw you in. Highly recommended!"

John Townsend, Ph.D.
Co-author of the New York Times bestselling Boundaries and Founder, Townsend Institute, and Townsend Leadership Program

This is an exceptional book that will leave an indelible mark on anyone who reads it. This captivating account of Denis' life journey, from a successful corporate executive to finding his true purpose in life, is a compelling story of personal transformation. Denis encourages readers to examine the things they fill their lives with and consider whether they are truly being fulfilled. It offers a compassionate and truthful approach to self-auditing, inviting readers to question the ideas that govern their lives and reset them on healthier foundations for true joy and indestructible wealth. Candid and illuminating, The Biggest Idea Ever is more than just a book - it's a blueprint for a flourishing life.

Virginie Helias
Chief Sustainability Officer, Procter & Gamble

I've been impressed with Denis as an executive, a pastor, and a friend. He lays out a practical roadmap to a life of peace, purpose, and significance. His story is vulnerable, adventurous, and written from the perspective of the marketplace where he excelled as a leader and coach. If you've given up on religion but still ache for more in your life and work, this book is on the money. Allow yourself to be guided by a strong man who has strong results.

Brian Tome
Senior Pastor Crossroads Church

A must read for all of us who are trying to balance family and career and find meaning, purpose, and happiness in our lives.

Carl H. Lindner III
CEO American Financial Group, CEO FC Cincinnati

Denis Beausejour excelled in the global business arena and brings a deft spiritual touch to those he mentors. I have experienced that personally. Every business leader will benefit from this book, regardless of where you are on the spiritual journey.

Dan Rajaiah
Director, Global Strategy & Operations, Mastercard

This story is so well-written and captivating. I was engaged in all the ups and downs, highs and lows, and his experiences, emotions, struggles, health issues, and spiritual journey from childhood to his great awakening. But what gripped my heart was Denis admitting to being blinded by the veil of self-sufficiency—such a great description. Denis maps out a practical transformation path for the reader. Take some time to sit with this book and listen. Hear the gentle wooing from God as Denis leads you through a life changing spiritual journey.

Danise DiStasi
Founder and CEO, Unleash Love, Author, Love Like Louie

Few have shared their life story in such a personal, authentic, and relevant way for others' benefit. Denis' unique perspective is fresh and compelling. Denis shares his life story in an honest and authentic way for the benefit of the next generation of business leaders. The Biggest Idea Ever includes practical spiritual truths to apply to your business and personal life in new and energizing ways. An entirely new take on character driven leadership.

Tom Blinn
Former P&G VP, Global Personal Health Care.

This book is a life-changing "transformational" story for YOU. It is loaded with practical wisdom that you will never hear from your boss or business friends. Denis is a "nobody from nowhere" who rose to the top marketing position in the world. While he was leading Marketing for Procter & Gamble, he went through a faith-driven transformation that helped him to become a "force for good" despite incredible personal failings that business leaders will relate to. Denis will help YOU to find hope and satisfaction at work, home, and with your friends. I promise YOU are about to become "transformed"!

Dr. Jim Bechtold
Chief Innovation Officer, The CEO Forum

After encountering Jesus, Denis, a successful business executive, was forever changed. In his soul-stirring, God-inspired, personal story, the reader discovers what it truly means to seek first the Kingdom of God and his righteousness and find everything in the process. A beautiful and compelling read reflecting the goodness and faithfulness of God.

Candy Marballi
Author, He Hears Her Voice,
and Retired President, The Prayer Covenant

Denis has had a profound impact on virtually every part of my life - my relationship with God, my marriage, and even my business. This book will do the same for everyone who reads it. The personal stories, wisdom, and life-changing principles in The Biggest Idea Ever are priceless. They will challenge, inspire, and equip you to live a life of meaning, purpose, and adventure.

Chris Ignizio
Co-Founder and Creative Director, Scope and Sequence

This is a dramatic story about changing the course of one's life. Denis is living proof that no one can understand the power of light without experiencing darkness. He brings powerfully fresh insight to man's modern-day search for meaning and ages-old messages from the Bible. While I have always found the Bible difficult to read, this book opens the Bible in understandable chunks and shows me practical ways to live freely and lightly. It encourages all of us to think long term and to "finish well" in pursuit of our life's purpose.

Tim Love
Author of Discovering Truth,
and Retired Vice-Chairman Omnicom Group

Providentially the calendars of two busy executives cleared for a retreat, and we have been friends ever since. We heard a talk about "Priorities" and tears began to flow as we realized ours needed serious repair. The Spirit moved mightily that weekend and lives were changed. Denis has been a friend, mentor, advisor, confidant, and example to me. You will be inspired greatly as you read his book. It will help you make your work and family life all it can be.

Michael Ducker
Retired President and CEO FedEx Freight

How amazing to see God at work. God wants to reach each person, including highly successful, highly capable business executives. What a fascinating story of God's mercy and redemption in Denis' life. This book is for any person in the middle of great business success who is wondering what is truly most important.

Steve Cesler
Retired Vice President - Sales, The Procter & Gamble Company

Denis challenges readers to rethink the good life, gaining knowledge, success, wisdom, security, and lasting wealth. If you are searching for more in life, I highly recommend this book. The Biggest Idea Ever is inspiring, thought provoking and widens our horizon to pursue the ultimate purpose of loving God and others in Jesus Christ. Denis humbly and courageously shares his challenges, failures, and breakthroughs. An awesome book!

SueLee Jin
Pastor Anderson Hills Salem Campus

This is a beautifully crafted description of the kingdom. With the heart of a pastor and the mind of an executive, Denis weaves wisdom and powerful stories to show us a new paradigm of purpose. His flair for honest, vivid, and thought-provoking insight gives power to the meaning of life – which is the genuine gift of this book.

John Morelock
Founder/CEO, Calvary Industries, Inc.

Denis was one of the most influential figures in the world of marketing, commanding the reins of P&G's global advertising strategy and budget. The Biggest Idea Ever chronicles his transformative journey from one of the highest echelons of the corporate world to a spiritual mentor, guiding many for personal and professional growth. His story is profoundly inspiring. His book is a treasure trove of wisdom where you can find the path to peace, purpose, and significance.

Pete Blackshaw
CEO Cintrifuse

I'm thankful for the energy, wisdom, and love you'll find in The Biggest Idea Ever. Many people write books from head knowledge and others from a combination of knowledge and experience, and it is easy to detect the difference. This book is the real deal. Readers who apply this book's message will discover the proven path to lasting transformation.

Ford Taylor
Founder FSH Consulting LLC,
Author of Relactional Leadership

This is a must read for the business leader struggling to find peace, purpose, meaning and margin in the fast paced, hectic corporate world. This is a personal story of transformation that anyone can experience. You will find a practical path to freedom and abundant life for yourself, your family, and your friends.

Si Pitstick
Executive Managing Director, Newmark Cincinnati

Contents

Part IV. How do I live it?

Foreword

One way to judge an idea is by how much you are willing to bet on it. This book is about the idea that broke my "big idea" meter. It's the story of how I bet my life on that idea and how it transformed my life, family, and work.

My odyssey from lower-middle-class Canada to becoming the youngest VP in Procter & Gamble's history was filled with big ideas and marketing wins.

But that was just the prelude to the real adventure.

In 1995, I nearly died in Japan's Great Hanshin Earthquake. In its traumatic wake, I discovered an entirely new world. It was like finding buried treasure.

Five years later, I left the pinnacle of the advertising world, risking stability and comfort to follow an irresistible adventure.

The Wall Street Journal and *Ad Age* chronicled my industry-baffling exodus.

So, what happened?

I found supernatural fuel for my marriage, family, leadership, and work. I discovered peace, purpose, and enduring significance.

If you are experiencing anxiety, fear, burnout, or you want more from life, this book is for you.

I believe my journey will spur you onward in yours. There is more available than we can possibly imagine.

Let's go after it together.

Denis Beauséjour
Cincinnati, Ohio

Chapter 1

Ideas Matter: Build Your Life on What Will Last.

"Tyranny cannot defeat the power of ideas."

~ Helen Keller

*"The mind, once stretched by a new idea,
never returns to its original dimensions."*

~ Ralph Waldo Emerson

Ideas are powerful. Good ones, and bad ones too.

What ideas are shaping your life?

The ideas we build our lives on directly impact the outcomes we experience. Let me illustrate with two examples from my story.

I was raised in the 1960s in a lower middle-class housing project in the east suburbs of Ottawa, Canada's capital. The community was bilingual, and the project was diverse, with families from Europe, India, Russia, and the United States. It was safe, friendly, and mostly made up of families with both parents working and living paycheck to paycheck.

After school, my three little sisters and I would get a snack and do homework with a babysitter or a neighbor until mom got home from work.

My mother an office manager for an aluminum supply business, and my dad was an insurance adjuster. They had high school educations and consequently fell behind the economic gains enjoyed by college graduates in the booming 60s economy.

We rented a two-bedroom townhouse, and I slept in a makeshift room in an unfinished basement. My dad had a car, and my mom took the bus to and from work. My mother lamented a loss of living standard compared to her childhood.

From an early age, mom talked about education. She was convinced that the way out of our constrained lifestyle was to get a great education. Her belief in this idea motivated her to invest heavily in our schoolwork. I felt her conviction.

She enrolled us in a French immersion school, believing this would accelerate our development. She made us rewrite sloppy homework, read books with us, and rewarded us lavishly when report cards were excellent.

The idea of a great education was her drumbeat.

We attended a new parochial school attached to our Catholic parish. As the fledgling school grew, there were imbalances of student numbers in each grade. They skipped me and a few others over grade 2 to make the grade 3 class the right size. Later, my grade 7 class was combined with the grade 8 class.

The grade 7-8 teacher was a renaissance man like Sidney Poitier in the film *To Sir with Love*. Mr. Sabourin took us to the symphony, museums, and government buildings. When I finished first in my class, they promoted me into high school.

I was 12 and mom was beaming.

In the middle of grade 9, we moved to Toronto. My mom looked for the best high school in the city and enrolled me there. The city and the learning language changed, but mom's message stayed the same—a great education will open doors!

It was a tough transition. It was one thing to be 5'2" with a brush-cut in suburban Ottawa. In Toronto, I felt like an alien, especially in gym class. The guy changing beside me on my first day was a physical specimen named Andy. He had long hair, had been shaving for a year, and had a hairy, muscular physique.

Gym class was a torture until I finally hit puberty in my sophomore year. For the rest of the time, Michael Power High School was a rich environment, loaded with Latin, Shakespeare, Spanish, Algebra, Sciences, a traveling debate team, and good friends.

Private school tuition meant that I needed to find a part-time job to help defray the expenses my parents could not cover. I babysat often, making 50 cents an hour. I was able to start working at McDonald's when I turned 14, making the princely sum of $1 an hour. This fulfilled the second of my mother's big ideas: hard work. She modeled a phenomenal work ethic.

I was making the Dean's list and working 30-40 hours a week, learning a ton from an outstanding manager named Jim. One of his many classics: "Those who know how will always work for those who know why." That pithy axiom has stuck with me and itself illustrates the power of ideas. (Later, I learned Jim was paraphrasing Ralph Waldo Emerson.)

As the time for college approached, I was invited to a reunion weekend at Queen's University by a good friend of my dad's. Stan and his wife Joanie were married the same time as my parents, moved in across the hall, and began a life-long friendship.

Stan graduated from Queen's Engineering and played football. While in Kingston, for the weekend, we met Stan's father-in-law. Alex Edmison was a judge and a Queen's Law grad who was very engaged in the University. He took a real interest in me.

That weekend, I decided Queen's would be my first choice for college. They had the country's best undergraduate business program. Later, I learned that my case was aided by an incredibly strong letter of recommendation from Alex.

Attending Queen's School of Business (now the Smith School of Business) was an exceptional experience. We engaged with a great faculty in small class sizes, group projects, case studies, and community consulting assignments. Queen's was my path to opportunity and growth.

At the same time, I worked 30-40 hours a week as a shift manager for the local McDonald's franchisee. This complemented my pursuit of a great education with an ethic of hard work.

The owner, Rick Hession, taught me tons about marketing and leadership, and he strongly suggested I pursue a career at P&G. He had cut his teeth in consumer packaged goods at Facelle-Royale and had observed P&G's excellence.

During my last year at Queen's, I was offered a fantastic brand management job at P&G in Toronto. It was exciting, had great upside potential, and was proof that education and hard work were the big ideas that would lead to success in life.

I'll come back to my career adventures later, but I want to stop here and ask you if you notice the gap in my ideology.

Education and hard work were important, but it took me a long time to realize that relationships were the key to my growth. I had a wealth of relational support and mentoring that I did not appreciate until much later.

At the top of the list is the profound impact of my mother's love, encouragement, and example. My grade 7-8 teacher opened the worlds of history and culture to me. My boss at McDonald's taught me to start with "why." Stan's friendship led to my university choice. Alex's letter of recommendation opened doors. Rick's example and coaching gave me a huge leg up.

Education and hard work were good ideas, but they were incomplete for long-term success. I had missed the value and power of good relationships.

I had been trained to hide my family's problems, and that also meant that I hid my own feelings, which stunted my relational growth. I needed to be more authentic and transparent and learn to cultivate relationships.

Sadly, I did not focus on this until much later in life.

A second example of the power of ideas relates to a very challenging time in my childhood that resulted in the adoption of a very harmful idea.

I played hockey for a local team in Ottawa. I was 11 years old, and our first game of the year was at an outdoor rink one night at 7 pm. My dad was supposed to come home after work with a new stick and a new pair of gloves for me. He did not come home until late that night. I was so angry.

My mom got a sitter and borrowed a car to take me to my game. I was so embarrassed to have to borrow a stick from someone, and I had to play with mittens instead of hockey gloves. I played through it and scored a hat-trick in a 3-0 win. Despite the win, I felt shame. My mom froze on the sidelines. I felt so bad for her. My dad had let us both down again!

I vowed that I would never let that happen again.

In Toronto, I played hockey for a travel team, which involved expenses for ice time, equipment, and travel. I needed some new equipment and fees for a tournament. I saved my McDonald's earnings and stopped involving my folks in my needs.

Only later did I realize I had taken a vow of self-sufficiency.

Not only did this impact my friendships and work relationships, but it also affected my marriage. My beliefs had led me to the unintended consequences of rejecting community, teamwork, trust, and interdependence.

These two examples illustrate how ideas really matter. This is true of the ideas behind our most intimate and personal beliefs, and the larger world of ideas and beliefs in which we navigate every day. I brought these core ideas into my career at P&G.

I started as a Brand Assistant on Pampers diapers. My first business trip was to staff the Pampers booth at a Baby Fair in Ottawa. I spent hours changing diapers and talking to mothers about their ideas and beliefs about their babies' needs.

At that time, cloth diapers ruled. Disposables were more convenient and sanitary but more expensive. Cloth diapers were seen as better for the baby's skin. This led us to focus on skin dryness improvements. The key belief we had to win on was superior baby care—mom's convenience was not enough.

Throughout my career, I learned how to better understand consumer beliefs and desires. Based on fresh insights, we developed new product, packaging, and advertising ideas which brought competitive advantage along with sales and profit growth.

The consumer was the boss, and everything hinged on knowing their habits and beliefs better than anyone.

A big new consumer insight translated into a new product or marketing idea could create new categories and redefine existing ones. Often, a well-crafted change in advertising could propel our brands to double-digit market share growth and dramatic profitability improvement.

P&G's marketing culture was full of passionate "consumer students" seeking to understand beliefs that would yield the next big idea for that business.

Pampers' advertising showing the benefit of superior dryness versus cloth diapers propelled market growth and our share, yielding double-digit growth over the next several years.

In Australia, a new campaign for Olay portrayed the impact of this highly efficacious skin care product in dramatic "mistaken age" commercials which eventually aired around the world. The brand grew by double digits and made Australia one of Olay's most developed and profitable markets.

In Japan, we studied the consumer's mindset about germs, looking at ways to grow our antibacterial soap brand called Muse. Through playground observation with moms, we learned about the everyday situations Japanese kids got into, like hands on urinals and digging in sandboxes used by cats. We showed how Muse protects children's health from moms' greatest worries, and the business grew dramatically.

In China, I spent a week living in a remote village so I could observe and dialogue with rural consumers. I was curious to see how they did laundry and how they brushed their teeth, and what their beliefs were about fabric and oral care. The challenges with food and dirt stains in clothes and the difficulty rinsing clothes outside in cold water led to a new Tide formula with enzymes that delivered superior cleaning.

The villagers believed their teeth were like porcelain, so they used stiff brushes and high suds toothpastes that delivered a clean feel. However, when they learned that their teeth were porous like a coral reef, and that Crest's fluoride formula filled in the gaps in the structure of their teeth, they flocked to Crest (which also delivered a clean feel). Fluoride efficacy was the new gold standard, leading to exceptional consumer satisfaction.

Ideas move people because they change beliefs. For better—and for worse! Let me give a few examples of great ideas I've found worthy of building my life on, and others I needed to discard.

Thirty years ago, I read *The Road Less Traveled* by Dr. M. Scott Peck.[1] His authentic sharing of his failures and relationship lessons had a big impact on me. He was part of the journey that led me to renounce my vow of self-sufficiency.

That book helped me root out bad ideas like hiding family secrets and replacing them with better ideas grounded in truth and reality, like authenticity and transparency and safe community. Don't we need that now more than ever?

Twenty years ago, I read *Changes That Heal* by Dr. Henry Cloud.[2] His description of the four key tasks of personal growth provided a framework for my life that is so helpful, I use it all the time in my family and my mentoring.

Dr. Cloud's first task is to learn to say yes in relationships, the healthy process of bonding or making healthy attachments. I missed this for much of my life, but Henry's book helped me take huge steps forward in my relationships.

Second, we need to learn to say no, setting healthy boundaries. Because my relationships were not deeply grounded, and I was a pleaser, I hated saying no. Learning to say no is crucial to personhood and to effective choices.

---

[1] Dr. Peck's follow up work *Further Along the Road Less Traveled* is also worth the extra effort. His book *Golf in the Spirit* is a brilliant exploration of a sport I love.

[2] This is Dr. Cloud's seminal work. His subsequent books explore each of these four tasks of growth. The most well-known is *Boundaries*, co-authored with Dr. John Townsend. Dr. Cloud has also developed an influential body of business books based on his consulting work with CEOs and boards. I recommend starting with his book *Integrity*.

Third, I needed to recognize that no one is all good or all bad, thus learning to accept imperfect people. I often saw people as all good or all bad. This led to being disappointed and to avoiding, rather than accepting of myself and others as works in progress.

And fourth, I needed to move into adulthood and into an equal footing with others. I assumed some people were above me and acted fearfully around them. I saw others below me, and proudly treated them as inferiors. Treating everyone as a respected peer brought great authority and confidence to my relationships.

Dr. Cloud's framework radically altered my life, marriage, parenting, and leadership.

One idea that is negatively impacting our culture is the delay of marriage. Recently, I read *Twelve Rules for Life—an Antidote to Chaos* by Dr. Jordan B. Peterson.[3] Peterson is encouraging a return to personal responsibility, especially encouraging young men to give up video games and to seek to become effective husbands and fathers that can build great families and productive careers.

His ideas are brilliantly coherent and have been a great resource in my mentoring work among young fathers who are seeking to grow, take responsibility and balance the challenges of family and career.

A related negative idea is that children are a big liability, costly, and a barrier to freedom. Some have even suggested that having children is an assault on the environment. I was affected by this thinking. I was concerned about my ability to give proper attention to my first two kids given my priority on career. My

---

[3] Dr. Peterson has also developed a very powerful personality test that can be taken as an individual and can also be shared with a spouse. He argues that personality is the critical variable to understand yourself and to maximize your work and interpersonal effectiveness. See understandmyself.com

wife Marianne stood firm on wanting four children, and thankfully I eventually yielded to her.

Because of the low birth rates in Western Europe, China, and Japan, nations are in grave danger of not being able to sustain their cultures. China saw the problem and finally reversed its one child policy, yet many believe they will never recover.

Japan is in such danger of economic collapse from low birth rates that high court judges recently denied the legalization of same sex marriages with the stated reasoning that these unions do not produce children.

Larger families can have a huge and positive impact on our culture if we will see kids as assets and critical members of our family teams.

To help integrate the structure of ideas I am building my life on, I have found a simple and yet very powerful model for a balanced life. It is called the five capitals.[4]

The model starts with financial capital, a pre-requisite for flourishing, measured in dollars and cents. However, many tend to focus on money and lose sight of the fact that we can accumulate so much more than financial capital.

Next is intellectual capital, which is even more powerful, because it measures the value of our ideas, the focus of this chapter. For example, one great idea can spawn a new business and quickly double our financial capital.

Next is physical capital, which is expressed in our resources of health and time. Health, time, and money tend to take turns being in short supply as we age. When we are young, we have

---

[4] For more details, please see fivecapitals.net and especially the book *Build a Better Life* by Brandon Schaefer.

health and time but less money. In middle years, we have money and health, but we are time starved. Later in life, we have money and time, but health becomes the issue. So physical capital has huge leverage. If we are not managing our health and time well, we will be ineffective intellectually and financially.

The next higher order capital is relational capital, which measures the depth and quality of our relationships. This is so powerful, because with the right people, we can offset our weaknesses and benefit from skills we don't have. Relationships have been the key to every breakthrough in my story.

The highest order capital is spiritual, measured in the faith we have and the wisdom and power that only faith can access. The beauty of the five capitals model is that in pursuing them holistically, we will always remain balanced.

In contrast, pursuing things like pleasure, prosperity, power, prestige, and position always leads to imbalance. Bad ideas produce bad fruit. Strong ideas blossom, and from humble beginnings they produce good fruit that endures.

That's why we need to build our lives on ideas that will stand the test of time.

Reflection question:

What idea has been the most valuable in your life so far?

Practical application:

List the ideas driving your life. Which are most fruitful? Which are not? What is confused? What is missing?

There is a body of wise ideas that will lead to a happy, productive, and fulfilling life. The sages call this the Good Life, the subject of our next chapter.

Chapter 2

The Good Life: Is Yours Worth Dying For?

*"Happiness then, is found to be something perfect and self-sufficient, being
the end to which our actions are directed."*

~ Aristotle

*"We hold these truths to be self-evident, that all men are created equal,
that they are endowed by their Creator with certain unalienable Rights,
that among these are Life, Liberty and the pursuit of Happiness."*

~ U.S. Declaration of Independence

What is the Good Life? Is that Good Life worth the cost to
obtain it? Is that life worth dying for?

The first glimpses we have of the Good Life come from our
parents and our family life. Think about the traditions of home and
your most important memories.

What was celebrated and valued? What was rejected?

I spent my winter Saturdays at the local ice rink, a five-minute
walk from our townhouse. The rink had a shed heated by a
wood-burning stove where we would lace up our skates and
warm up throughout the day. Today, the smell of burning wood
still triggers my happy rink memories!

I played pick-up hockey with my buddies inside the boards, and
my three little sisters Patty, Marie, and Michelle figure skated
with their friends on a wide oval belt of ice that wrapped around
the boards. We walked home for lunch, which usually consisted
of hot chocolate and peanut butter and jam sandwiches.

Then back to the rink!

The air was crisp and clear. You could feel the cold air stick inside your nostrils. I imagined myself playing for my beloved Montréal Canadiens (aka the Habs). The games were dominated by the older teenage kids, and my bliss was often interrupted by a slap shot to the shins or a body check I wasn't expecting. But scoring on a breakaway made everything right!

After dinner, we watched *Hockey Night in Canada*. The girls could stay up for the first period, and I was allowed to watch the second, and occasionally the third. These were the best times with my Dad. He shared his memories and experiences following the Habs. Once while in Montréal, we attended a practice and got to meet some of the coaches and players.

In the summers, I went to a boys' camp near Sherbrooke, Quebec, for three weeks. The first time, I was only six years old, and very homesick. By the following year, I was eager to stay longer, and eventually spent six weeks at camp every summer until my second year of high school. This was where I learned to swim, run, make fires, do laundry, pick blueberries, and hike using a map and compass. There, I discovered I had leadership ability.

Throughout the school year, we followed a strong routine of homework right after school. We could only go out to play once that was all done and checked. The routine was solid, priorities were clear, and the rhythm of life was predictable.

We celebrated the French-Canadian Christmas by wrapping presents, going to midnight mass, followed by "Réveillon" – staying up to open gifts and eat. The idea was to sleep in on Christmas morning. Of course, that didn't work out too well with an excited young kid eager to practice slap shots with his new hockey stick.

On Saint Patrick's Day, we honored mom's Irish heritage. She dyed her hair green and served green pancakes with green butter and green maple syrup. I was sent to school with a green paper shamrock pinned onto my green sweater. The shamrock featured my two middle names and modified last name: Francis Paddy O'Beausejour.

This was the healthy part of my upbringing. I gained a sense of where I had come from as a bilingual kid with a French and Irish heritage. I was taught to seek a great education and work hard. I learned to enjoy the simple things like skating fast and scoring goals, cold rosy cheeks, piping hot chocolate, and long summers away growing into adolescence.

But it did not last.

Things started falling apart in my dad's world. He drank to excess and often came home late. He discovered he was decent at bumper pool and began to gamble. That led to more late-night arrivals, arguments, and tears of disappointment for mom.

My mom took over the finances and put dad on a budget. That seemed to help. But the drinking continued, at times including my mom. Add heavy smoking, and I was old enough to see the changes. Late nights, blank mornings, and growing chaos.

Some weekend mornings I'd wake first and find the living and dining room full of dishes, empty bottles, and full ashtrays. I noticed burn holes in our furniture. I cleaned up and aired out the place. Then I made breakfast for my sisters, and we ate together while mom and dad slept in. It was a weird feeling of instability mixed with sadness and a bit of fear. We saw what was happening, but we did not have the tools or the resources to bring about change.

My Good Life had morphed into something very unhealthy.

My dad's drinking led to more gambling and eventually to the loss of his job. Our finances were always on the brink. Then one day my dad left, and my mom had no idea where he went.

Mom finally located dad in Toronto.

He was looking for a better job. She decided we would move there and try for a fresh start. We found a new apartment and settled into new schools. Things were stable for a while, but the cycle of job losses and financial struggles continued with dad's drinking. I could see the stress on my mom's face.

As our teenage years rolled on, we all spent more time with our friends, school activities, and part-time jobs. Dad's old friend Stan offered him a position in a new company he had started, and things seemed to stabilize.

When I graduated from high school, my dad helped me buy a used Volkswagen Beetle. He knew used cars from his prior work, and I felt loved and supported. As I headed off to college, I was cautiously optimistic for my family.

I decided to stay in Kingston for the summer between my first and second year at Queen's to work at McDonald's. My roommate went home, so mom asked if my sister Patty could come and live with me and work at McDonald's. She was not flourishing in Toronto, so I readily agreed. We hit a few bumps but ended up having a great summer together.

The next summer, I took a job as a loans and collections officer in Toronto to get some experience in finance. Living temporarily at home, I once again saw my dad's chaotic life and its effects on my mom and sisters.

Thankfully I gained a glimpse of what a healthy family life can be through a college girlfriend who regularly invited me for Sunday dinner with her family in Kingston. Mary Kate had 7 siblings, and those dinners at their huge dining room table were an oasis for my soul. Great food served with love, playful banter back and forth between siblings, with parents sharing wisdom, encouragement, and correction over the events of the week. My family's table culture was shaped by that experience.

By the time I graduated from college and started my career at P&G in 1978, life at home had further deteriorated and my sisters had decided to move out and live with friends. My sisters had to settle for a year or two of community college because of finances. They all had to work to pay the bills. It would take years to process our pain as we tried to find the Good Life.

In early 1980, I met Marianne McKeen at P&G.

That changed everything!

Marianne was interviewing for a Brand management position at P&G, and I was a last-minute substitute to be her dinner host. Her resume was beyond amazing - the MBA student body President with straight A's, a decorated track and volleyball athlete, and a former Miss Canada. I was curious to meet her. What would she be like?

She ordered scotch and soda at a time when most women drank wine spritzers. Marianne was the most humble and down to earth woman I had ever met, and we had a million things in common. I knew I wanted to marry her in the first 40 minutes.

I was mesmerized.

Marianne landed the job the next day, and our relationship progressed over the spring and summer by long distance. She started at P&G in the late summer, and we were able to see each other most days. I was relieved to learn that she was starting to feel the same way about me.

That fall, my dad had to have major surgery to remove half his pancreas. It was the turning point in his health, and he lost about 75 pounds. I'll never forget introducing Marianne to my dad at the hospital and watching her turn white as a sheet. It was not the intro I hoped for.

Marianne and I were engaged at Christmas and married September 12, 1981. It was a joyful time despite my dad's decline. My sisters also married over the next two years. We celebrated together, glad that we were all getting a taste of the Good Life.

My career at P&G was accelerating and so was my family. I had a lead role in a corporate strategy project that produced significant improvement in P&G Canada's results. Our first son Denis was born in Toronto in 1985 and Michael followed in early 1987. My sisters also started their families. I was so happy.

Unfortunately, from that point until his death five years later, dad continued to experience illness and job losses. He and my mom separated. Dad continued in a cycle of rehab and relapse. He lived with us for a few months, but when he violated our no smoking rule and nearly burned our house down, we had to ask him to leave. Mom lived with my youngest sister Michelle and finally found peace and stability.

In June 1988, I was promoted to lead P&G's business in Sydney, Australia. It was a huge opportunity and a fantastic place to live and explore. We flew mom out in 1989 and had a wonderful six-week visit, during which we welcomed our third son Patrick. She enjoyed just being a happy grandmother. Later, we flew dad out for a six-week visit. I think my parents may have enjoyed the most peaceful time in their lives with us in beautiful Sydney. They passed away soon after visiting us, one year apart.

Neither made it to 60.

Mom died of emphysema and a panic attack in a Florida hospital while visiting her best friend. I was only able to talk with her on the phone once. That was a huge loss. Marianne embraced my pain and helped me grieve well. My mother's love, support, and high standards shaped me deeply. She kept our family afloat despite her own grief; she was so courageous.

Her fierce love gave me a shot at the Good Life.

About a year later, Dad was hospitalized suddenly while we were on vacation in Hawaii. I left for Toronto, and Marianne went back to Australia. Dad had been living a homeless lifestyle and was never able to stop drinking. He had burned every bridge with his family and friends.

I visited him for several hours daily over two weeks. We sorted out the issues in our relationship and extended forgiveness. I learned more about his difficult childhood and the impact of his mother's death when he was five years old. The lack of connection with his dad and stepmom affected him deeply.

I felt a wave of empathy for my dad. As I got ready to return to Australia, we hugged and said, "I love you." Unfortunately, he was not emotionally able to reconcile with my sisters. He passed away 10 days after I returned to Australia. We had a service at the hospital and buried him with mom in Sherbrooke.

These experiences shaped my view of the Good Life. They made me acutely aware of the consequences of bad choices.

Great thinkers have wrestled for centuries with what constitutes a Good Life, and there is no better starting point than the philosopher Aristotle (384-322 BC). Aristotle learned under Plato and taught Alexander the Great. His book *Nicomachean Ethics* outlines his teaching on the Good Life.[5]

Aristotle concluded that the good life consists in the possession, over the course of a lifetime, of all those things that are good for us. He identified three categories of "human goods" that are required for the Good Life.

First, bodily goods including health, vitality, vigor, and pleasure. Second, external goods including food, drink, shelter, clothing, and sleep. And third, goods for the soul including knowledge, skill, love, friendship, aesthetic enjoyment, self-esteem, honor, and virtue. The Good Life is attaining and maintaining the proper balance of these human goods. It requires a life-long commitment to learning and improvement.

Virtue plays a central role in Aristotle's thinking. A disposition to virtue provides an internal compass and habits that prioritize best choices. Aristotle identified virtues of thinking (such as knowledge, wisdom, and judgment) and doing (such as courage, justice, humility, and generosity). He saw virtue as an ideal he called the golden mean. For example, courage is the golden mean between the extremes of cowardice and recklessness.

Aristotle used the word *eudaimonia* to describe the Good Life, and although this word is often translated as happiness, it means living well or flourishing. Flourishing is objective - it depends on our body and physical things in the world around us, not just our beliefs, feelings, or transcendent experiences.[6]

---

[5] In case you are curious about the name of Aristotle's book, Nicomachus was the name of his father and his son. There are many approachable English translations. Check out Irwin's third edition (2019) which has a lot of study aids, or Bartlett and Collins (2012).

[6] Flourishing is more than a positive mental state, such as pleasure, good mood, peace of mind, or satisfaction from having our preferences met, although those can be a byproduct of flourishing. Also, idea of earthly flourishing is consistent with the idea of transcendence. For a

Aristotle recognized that circumstances could impede our flourishing. He believed flourishing requires a good environment created by the state, in which all citizens can flourish. As I write this book, the people of Ukraine and Russia are unable to flourish because of one badly flawed leader. This is sadly normal.

My friend, Jack Painter, sees a connection between flourishing and rights. He believes rights protect the freedom to flourish by protecting self-direction, which is both a means to flourishing and a key feature of all forms of flourishing.[7]

Jack believes this approach to rights is consistent with our country's founding ideal that we would have rights to life, liberty, and the *pursuit of happiness.* [8]

The topic of happiness and flourishing has been the subject of numerous studies. One amazing source of wisdom on the topic is Harvard's Grant study underway since the mid-1940s.

George Vaillant directed the study for 55 years and published his summary of findings in 2012 in the landmark book *The Triumphs of Experience.*[9] The researchers developed an integrated measure of flourishing that included physical health, income, quality of marriage and relationships, work achievements, social recognition, and emotional health.

Vaillant concluded that early childhood experiences with at least one close loving parent or relative predicted a strong ability to

---

discussion of the views of Thomas Aquinas on earthly flourishing, see McMahon, Darrin M. *Happiness: A History.* New York, New York: Grove Press, 2006, 122-133.

[7] Self-direction is critical to flourishing because flourishing is not just possessing and using good things but the process of living intelligently, which requires self-directed conduct.

[8] Jack Painter is a retired lawyer and well-known speaker on liberty and the proper role of government. Keep an eye out for his forthcoming book on rights. You can access some of Jack's writing and speeches at JackPainter.com.

[9] The "Triumphs of Experience" chapter on the effects of alcohol abuse was especially powerful considering my dad's experiences. See also Vaillant's book *Aging Well.*

thrive. This was encouraging to me because it did not require an idyllic home life. It also showed that you can teach an old dog new tricks, as many of the men adjusted, changed, and continued to thrive into their eighties and nineties.

Some started out with very difficult upbringings and did not recover until their fifties and sixties. Men whose lives were destroyed by alcohol were able to get sober and turn their lives around. Others who were divorced early were able to remarry and enjoy happy marriages. Some discovered new ethical and moral truth, others experienced spiritual renewal.

The study proves we can choose wisdom and find the Good Life even after things have gone badly. It validates continual learning and a lifestyle committed to wisdom, and moral and ethical growth. But while this is true for 260 men, of which few are still living in their 90s, is it still broadly accessible today? And what is that moral and ethical knowledge?

Dallas Willard (1935-2013), who was the chair of the Philosophy Department at the University of Southern California, spent much of his life studying ethics and morality.

He pointed out how we have lost many of the foundations of ethical and moral truth that once underpinned our great universities and our society. He highlights the teachings of Jesus and traces their impact on philosophical thought over the past 2,000 years, and their relevance in today's intellectual academy.

In his book *The Divine Conspiracy*[10] Willard shares a story of a middle-class student at Harvard who was belittled for her need to work cleaning student rooms to make ends meet. She was propositioned for sex by a wealthy student from her ethics and morality classes.

---

[10] Also, I highly recommend Willard's *Renovation of the Heart* and *Hearing God.*

She went to her professor for help, but he was not able or willing to denounce the behavior, or to provide the specific ethical and moral knowledge the offending student needed.

She left Harvard in frustration. In her exit interview, she asked why they were learning about ethics but not being held accountable to behave ethically. Willard concludes that the Harvard faculty, and most of our universities, must face the fact that: "There is now no recognized moral knowledge upon which moral development could be based."[11]

Willard contrasts this with Harvard professor George Palmer speaking in 1929: "Ethics is certainly the study of how life may be full and rich, and not, as is often imagined, how it may be restrained and meager. Those words of Jesus, announcing that he had come in order that people might have life and have it abundantly, are the clearest statement of the purposes of both morality and religion."[12] Willard adds: "That such a statement would be professional suicide today speaks volumes about where we now stand."[13]

Quoting the Sermon on the Mount, Willard shows how Jesus answers the question of what the Good Life is, and how one can live that life. Willard points out that this text is filled with specific and practical moral and ethical teaching, including injunctions to forgive others, to be like a light, how to order relationships, how to pray for others, a call to radical generosity, avoiding hypocrisy, and his famous golden rule.

Willard emphasizes one of the main points of Jesus' teaching: that this life of moral and ethical integrity is available to all, regardless of our race, gender, intellectual abilities, or socio-

---

[11] Dallas Willard, *The Divine Conspiracy*, 3.
[12] George Palmer, *The Field of Ethics*, 1929, 213.
[13] Willard, The Divine Conspiracy, 407.

economic status. And it comes with a guarantee that those who follow his teaching will find themselves weathering the storms of a chaotic world.

The power of these truths has been documented by multitudes of people in stunning biographies of the Good Life despite persecution, wars, and even death.

That's why we must ask ourselves if we are willing to die for the Good Life. This is not a theoretical question. Most of us would be willing to die to protect our children from harm.

I recently walked through the graveyards of Normandy and wept thankfully for the many young men willing die to protect our freedom. There was so much power and dignity in their choice, and their refusal to accept tyranny.

This was the heart of the famous speech by William Wallace in Mel Gibson's film *Braveheart*.

Many like him, including William Wilberforce, Dietrich Bonhoeffer, Winston Churchill, Richard and Sabina Wurmbrand, Martin Luther King Jr. and Rosa Parks have gladly faced conflict and death rather than compromise their vision of the Good Life.

Isn't that the ultimate test of the Good Life, a life so valuable that it is worth dying for?

Reflection question:

What is your definition of the Good Life?

Practical application:

What do you want to be remembered for? What do you hope will be said about you at your funeral?

Throughout life, it's normal to compare where we are to where we want to be. It is not unusual to have moments of reckoning as we see gaps between our goals and our reality. How will we handle these gaps?

Chapter 3

Reckoning: Confronting Reality.

"Life is not a problem to be solved, but a reality to be experienced."

~ Soren Kierkegaard

*"No one can take away my freedom
to choose how I will react to my circumstances."*

~ Viktor Frankl

The life we are aiming for often collides with the life we have. I call these moments of reckoning. I've had several, and I bet you have too. How we choose to use these crucial moments will determine more than we can imagine.

My first reckoning with reality came at age 6 when I heard about the assassination of John F. Kennedy on November 22, 1963. It was a shocking event blasted globally on television. That day I first felt evil—unspeakable evil that scared me, and all the adults around me. The world was stunned.

Soon after the news on JFK, I threw a rock at a kid who bullied me and ran away. I hit him on the back of the head. He was not badly hurt, but I got a serious spanking. I realized that I too could be violent. I was part of the problem. I felt deep shame and fear.

I experienced anger and retaliated against bullies many other times. Sometimes I took my anger out on my sisters, and occasionally at the hockey rink. I was introduced to pornography around age 13, and that produced my first experiences of lust. Alcohol and marijuana followed when I was 15.

There are so many distractions from the Good Life!

Thankfully, I survived high school and college without major reckonings. My P&G career in Toronto was mostly filled with successes, and that pattern continued in Australia.

The launch of Pert 2-in-1 took us to leadership in the haircare market. We achieved strong market share gains on our established brands like Olay and Vicks, driven by improved product offerings and better advertising. The business was booming.

I had just been elected P&G's youngest Vice President when my first professional moment of reckoning took place. Despite great test market results on Pampers, our national launch was blunted by our competition's rapid product improvement, price reductions, and aggressive promotion. Our imported product costs soared due to exchange rate changes. The result was a loss of $10 million.

I had to own the fiasco, discontinue the brand, and make major changes to restore our financial performance and retail credibility. After a time of soul searching and analysis, our team developed a new strategy to focus on our most profitable categories, and a new product supply system to reduce costs while improving cash flow and customer service.

By facing reality, I made changes that restored momentum and trust. I could have blamed it on my team, the competitor, or currency instability, but making excuses never leads to lasting change. In his business classic *Good to Great*,[14] Jim Collins calls leaders to "confront the brutal facts" without losing hope. I grew as a leader by facing my mistakes and applying what I learned. In just four years, we profitably grew the business five-fold.

Moments of reckoning crash into our lives in hundreds of ways. You might have been blindsided by a spouse seeking divorce.

---

[14] See jimcollins.com for more resources. Also, his previous book *Built to Last*, co-authored with Jerry Porras, is a great read for stoking vision and strategic insight.

Maybe a friend ended your relationship suddenly. A natural disaster may have ruined your property. It could be the death of a loved one, the suicide of a sibling, losing a job, filing for bankruptcy, or being charged with a DUI.

These moments hurt, but they present opportunities.

If we face these moments without putting our heads in the sand, failures can teach us. How we respond will determine whether we repeat mistakes or grow into new levels of effectiveness. The keys are to know who we are, to forgive ourselves and others, and to not let shame take hold. The *Top Gun* films speak powerfully about growing through moments of reckoning.

In the first film, Maverick is accidentally sucked into a flat spin and can't control his F-14. His radar-intercept officer Goose ejects violently into the plane's canopy and is killed instantly. Maverick is crushed at the loss of his best friend and almost washes out of the Navy in shame and indecision. Viper tells Maverick that his disgraced father was the hero in a highly classified mission. A trusted father-figure removes the shame that Maverick carried in his family identity and frees him to move on and excel.

In the second film, Goose's son Rooster is the new red-hot pilot, and Maverick is now the veteran instructor. Rooster distrusts Maverick. Rooster must fight the pain of his fatherlessness and deal with reality—his own life and the lives of others are on the line. Maverick puts a fatherly trust in Rooster's skill, and his confidence surges. Rooster learns to fly without fear.

My next moment of reckoning had to do with our family planning. Marianne wanted four kids, and ideally a girl. After three sons, we wondered if a girl was in the cards. We had been in discussion for months as to whether we would even try for a fourth child. I felt that our lives were so full.

While visiting Sydney, future CEO John Pepper heard about these deliberations one night during a team dinner with our spouses. John had three boys, then was blessed with a girl who is the apple of his eye. John, in his fatherly way, strongly encouraged me to go for a daughter.

Marianne followed with a P&G-style one-page memo entitled "The Fourth." It was a moment of reckoning in our marriage. We talked more, and I finally heard Marianne's heart. We bought a book on choosing the sex of your baby and went for it.

Marianne got pregnant quickly. She was looking forward to another couple of years in Australia when I was asked to lead the Health and Beauty Care business in Japan. It was a whirlwind, but we moved to Japan in June 1992.

Our daughter Mariel was born in February 1993. John Pepper sent warm congratulations. Marianne still claims that my greatest quality is that I am teachable. Slow, but teachable.

Life in Japan was very different. We worked hard at learning the language and understanding the culture. Marianne learned Japanese painting, we climbed Mount Fuji, and we traveled throughout the country. We got to know several Japanese families and tried every style of Japanese cuisine. We fell in love with Japan.

The hard lessons learned in Australia paid huge dividends in Japan. In the first two and half years, our business tripled, and our profits grew eight-fold. Our division led the world in sales and profit growth behind new brand launches, new advertising campaigns, and a new product supply system that had yielded amazing results in Australia. My team in Japan was highly energized, creative, and working together with trust. The young Japanese managers were growing as leaders, and my expat leaders were firing on all cylinders.

All that changed in the early hours of Tuesday, January 17, 1995.

I returned from meetings in Cincinnati the night before and was up at 4 am. for a jetlag run. I showered quietly and walked a few hundred yards across Rokko Island to my office around 5 am. At 5:46 a magnitude 7.2 earthquake unleashed incredible damage. The Great Hanshin Earthquake was the most powerful ever recorded, surpassing the 1906 San Francisco quake.

We were only a mile from the epicenter.

I was on my way back to my office on the 22nd floor, holding a hot cup of coffee, when the tremor started. For 22 seconds the building shook violently, and I was thrown to the ground. A large steel bookshelf holding a display of our brands crashed inches from my head. Office equipment was strewn everywhere. I heard the building's steel girders wincing like a large violin being played badly. One girder snapped loudly. Then the shaking stopped.

The 30-storey building teetered like a battered heavyweight boxer. Two 30,000-gallon water cisterns at the top of the building, designed to counter-sway in high typhoon winds, were knocked off their moorings, flooding each of the two stairwells. Outside, fires burned all over the hills of Kobe. There were 7,000 deaths, 43,000 injured, and 35,000 buildings down.

I was disoriented and numb. I laid there for several minutes.

I finally got up and started thinking. There was no power and the phones were dead. I worked my way down the flooded staircases and got to the basement. The only other person on site was the security guard. He had fainted as a concrete pillar vaporized down to the steel girders in front of him. He was slowly coming to. After helping him get oriented, we walked out of the building and headed to our homes.

I walked to our apartment building and began walking up to the 28th floor where we lived. On the 20th floor I heard my son Denis say, "I'm glad none of us were hurt." We reunited and headed for the ground floor.

Chaos reigned. Sirens blared and people milled about, wondering what to do next. Over the next few hours, assured that there were no tsunamis coming, we moved to the kids' two-story school on the island which had not been damaged like the high-rise buildings.

Hundreds of expats from P&G and other companies huddled together, and we began making plans to evacuate our families. All four bridges to Rokko Island were unusable. On day two, an intrepid CNN crew landed by chopper on Rokko Island. As the senior P&G guy on the scene, I gave an interview that allowed me to reassure concerned relatives and ask for help.

It was a war zone.

On day three, AG Lafley, our head of Asia, was able to return from China, and he rolled up his sleeves, sleeping with the troops on the school's couches as we worked to figure out next steps. Helicopters delivered food and water to the 600 expats and 15,000 locals who lived on the island. On day four, a supplier provided boats so we could transfer everyone to hotels in Osaka.

At the hotel, we received group therapeutic debriefings from seismic trauma experts sent from the USA. Shortly after, we sent our families to their home countries because our houses were unlivable. Marianne and the kids flew to Canada and spent six weeks there. Managers stayed behind, living in an Osaka hotel, and working from temporary office space.

The earthquake triggered all kinds of responses. One of our managers committed suicide. Some expat managers left and went home, deciding to look for new jobs elsewhere. Our local salespeople went out on scooters to help injured customers.

For several weeks, we worked crazy hours and tried to put things back together. I was still sleeping fully clothed with shoes on as aftershocks hit Osaka. The only normalcy I could find was in work, in late evening dinners with co-workers and, unfortunately, too much to drink.

As families returned and we got somewhat back to normal, AG asked me to move to China. I thought my next assignment would be to run the Japanese business since I understood the culture so well and had such strong results. Little did I know what was ahead of me.

We spent the spring of 1995 getting ready to move, packing up our disheveled apartment, looking for schools, and saying goodbye to our friends. Quite a few of us were transferred out, perhaps a good thing for trauma recovery.

As all this was going on, I began an audit of my life.

The near-death trauma brought so much loss and disruption. In the quake's aftermath I finally saw that my success in Japan had come with a much bigger cost than I was aware of.

I added responsibility for Asia's health care business about 18 months before the quake. I traveled a lot, and work took priority. I became an absentee dad. I was prone to drink and eat to excess. I was unfaithful to Marianne.

I was nowhere close to living the Good Life. I needed a reboot.

Our move to Hong Kong in June 1995 was a positive step. It was good to get away from the raised Kobe expressway that had fallen over on its side, which was my daily reminder of death.

Hong Kong was still under British rule, so most spoke English in addition to Cantonese. The city was vibrant.

Our new home was a five-level townhouse built onto the side of a cliff with stunning ocean views, which brought some beauty into the wreckage of our lives. We had our own swimming pool and a large outdoor patio with a basketball hoop. There were nice parks in our gated community, and the kids could ride their bikes safely to visit friends.

The kids settled in well at the International school and enjoyed a rotation of recreational team sports. Marianne was happy to have Vicki, a wonderful live-in amah from the Philippines to help her with cooking, cleaning, and laundry. Marianne quickly found a spiritual community to connect with.

During the last few months in Japan and the first few in Hong Kong, I realized Marianne was undergoing some significant changes. She was less hurried and frazzled. She had more available time—I used to have to book a date with her weeks in advance.

Marianne was serene despite all our chaos and losses. She took the quake and six weeks in Canada in stride. She was sad about leaving Japan, but embraced the move to Hong Kong and planned it beautifully. She was more present and resilient than ever.

I was jealous. Marianne had found peace.

I found her more attractive than ever and more fun to be with. She was empathetic and encouraging. Our date nights in Hong Kong were an oasis. I felt so loved.

The work in China was refreshing. My new boss Dimitri Panayotopoulos was visionary and relational. The young Chinese managers we were hiring from the best local universities were bright and hungry. They were excited to be part of a global company with high standards and great training. The challenge of understanding consumers and introducing new brands like Tide and Crest to the world's largest market was a dream assignment in many ways.

While the family spent time in Canada over the summer, I dove in and traveled to visit each of our joint ventures. The rhythm of the week was to take the train to Guangzhou Sunday night and be ready for meetings Monday morning.

We met with our partners, which included the representatives of Hutchison-Whampoa, our partner based in Hong Kong, the Communist Party members of the Bureau of Light Industry, the local factory manager and his team, and the P&G managers. The all-day meetings included reviews of finance, marketing, production, upstream product development, the latest consumer research updates, and human resources planning.

Monday night, we flew to Chengdu for meetings Tuesday. After that, meetings in Huzhou on Wednesday. Tianjin on Thursday and Beijing on Friday. Then home to Hong Kong.

Our travel team included four or five senior managers, two secretaries, and two translators. After each day's travel, it was not unusual to have our own meetings in the hotels. We debriefed, handled communications with Cincinnati and the Asia headquarters in Kobe, and followed up with our local P&G teams.

I brought Marianne on my weekly China trip once so she could see the sights and understand what I was doing. With breakfast at 7, lunch with our partners and late dinners, phone calls and meetings as late as 1:30 am, one trip was all she needed.

Weekends were a time to recharge and have quality time with our kids. Aside from hearing about test results, schoolwork faxes back and forth, and phone calls, I missed much of my kids' lives. As the weeks passed, the business excitement faded, and I started feeling exhausted.

By late November 1995, it was obvious that I was not fully recovered from the earthquake. The 80+ hour work weeks felt unsustainable. I was experiencing dissonance about my life, priorities, and future. I poured out my heart to Marianne. She listened empathetically and grasped my situation.

Marianne knew we needed a change of pace. She had the great idea to spend Christmas 1995 and New Year 1996 in Australia and New Zealand. For three weeks, we soaked in the stunning beauty of each country, with hikes, beach swims, and dinners with old friends.

The kids loved the change from Hong Kong, and it was balm on my soul to spend quality time with my family. Denis was 10, Michael was 8, Patrick was 6, and Mariel was almost 3. It was so good to be together - it felt like a long hug.

One day, we were hiking the Franz Josef glacier on the south island of New Zealand. In the glorious sunshine with the loudly creaking ice river below us, I had another moment of reckoning. I realized these kids were at a crucial age and were not getting what they needed.

As the post-earthquake audit of my life continued, I confronted the brutal facts. I was unsure what to do next. My life in China moved at the speed of light with little quality thinking time. I loved the people I worked with and the business opportunities. But I was not able to keep going and be true to the changes I knew needed to be made.

Team Beausejour needed a better way.

Reflection question:

Where is your current reality at odds with your vision and goals?

Practical application:

What next step can you take to address the gap?

My search for a better way came with surprising signposts.

Chapter 4

Signposts: Looking for a Better Way.

"There is a better way for everything. Find it."

~ Thomas Edison

*"Whoever views the world at fifty
the same way they did at twenty has wasted thirty years."*

~ Muhammad Ali

I started asking myself the questions I'd ask when exploring a new marketing strategy for a faltering brand. Could there be a better way to meet consumer needs? What are their unmet needs? What new sources of insight could shift our thinking?

I asked myself why was I on earth? Education and hard work were not enough. I needed a new grid and tools that would help me find balance and purpose.

I went back to *The Road Less Traveled* and read Scott Peck's follow-up book *Further Along the Road Less Traveled*. I was drawn to Peck's honesty and wisdom. He helped me realize that spirituality was a missing dimension of my life.

Marianne was changing, and I felt irresistibly drawn by her spiritual journey. I decided to add some Bible reading, so I threw Marianne's pocket King James New Testament into my briefcase for airplane reading.

One Friday on the way home, I reached the point where I could not process any more Nielsen summaries, business reviews, or capital proposals. I put all my mail in my briefcase and pulled out the pocket New Testament. The flight from Beijing to Hong

Kong was a bit of a sanctuary. I read and sipped on a drink with my earphones tuned to classical music.

I found the first few chapters of Matthew's Gospel quite familiar—it was like attending midnight mass at Christmas. The nativity story was filled with angels, dreams, and narrow escapes. It reminded me of my childhood and sparked reflection.

How wild is the idea that God became a human being? Imagine an all-powerful God breastfeeding, learning to walk, being toilet trained, losing teeth, and going through puberty. He lived in obscurity until he was about 30, then stepped into history.

When I read about the temptations of Jesus in the desert, things got very personal.

Jesus fasting 40 days sounded impossible. I had little discipline when it came to food, drink, and sex. My appetites owned me. I couldn't imagine the self-control Jesus demonstrated, especially when he had the power to turn stones into fresh hot bread!

I read about how Jesus was challenged to throw himself off the temple so his angels could rescue him. I could see how tempting it would be for Jesus to get instant notoriety. In Japan, I was well known and respected. In China, I was still unknown. That was hard to get used to. Appearances were still driving me.

When offered all the Kingdoms of the world in return for his worship, Jesus had unswerving loyalty to his Father. In my unbridled ambition, I had traded life and family for success at work. I had no idea how to pivot without serious impact on Marianne and the kids.

Appetites, appearances, and ambition were ruling me. The signposts were obvious.

My identity was wrapped up in my work. I was the brash young kid from Canada who had rocketed into senior leadership of one of the world's most successful companies. I was determined to lift myself out of poverty and to be a success. But I was insecure without the recognition and admiration of others. My friendships were primarily tied to my work, taking precedence over my family, extended family, and my old friends. I had no boundaries.

My identity was tied up in titles, sales and profit numbers, advertising awards, stock options, and my ranking within the profit centers of the P&G world. In Japan, loyalty to companies is so high that when people introduce themselves, they start with their company name!

"Of P&G, Beausejour I am." Work was my identity!

Achievements were the meaning of my life. Winning market share leadership in a new category, launching successful new brands, and beating my profit forecasts were the hallmarks of my life's meaning. I was all about achievement.

Even my life's purpose was work. In 1987, P&G's CEO John Smale and future CEO John Pepper introduced a new Statement of Purpose as part of the 150th anniversary of the company's founding in 1837. It codified the company's purpose and operating principles. This was crucial to retain our DNA as we expanded into so many new countries and cultures.

I focused so much of my passion on my work. I began to see how my pride, marital unfaithfulness, and absent fathering left my family unprotected.

I realized that I found my true security in the compensation and benefits at P&G. I was making more money than I ever dreamed possible. Stock options brought unimagined wealth.

On top of that, we had a fabulous health care plan, profit-sharing retirement plans, and first-class travel. Our apartment in Japan and our townhouse in Hong Kong provided multi-million-dollar luxury that was light-years from my childhood experience.

These things became my security. My vow of self-sufficiency and my commitment to education and hard work were in full bloom. P&G was my identity, purpose, and security. I found my sense of destiny in my work, believing that my achievements would be my legacy - maybe in some hall of fame somewhere in the future.

Yet in all these vitally important matters, I lived like a captive. In all the great possibilities that life offers us, I had become a one-dimensional human being. I was living for myself and had crammed all my life's focus into my job.

No wonder I felt disoriented by the earthquake—it brought the reality of death and chaos into my central hope. The tremor had smashed the idol of my success and career game plan.

I was now in a new country, with lots of unanswered questions. I had all that I had most valued, but much like a competitor in the great hot-dog eating contest at Coney Island, I had finally reached my limit on work. That signpost was clear.

I knew my life was broken, but I had no idea what grid to use to start over. How would I re-order my priorities without financial disaster? But I was increasingly aware that my selfish perspective and behavior was deeply wrong.

I felt the weight of guilt pressing on me almost every day. I turned to the New Testament once again, looking for a signpost of a better way.

On cue, I was rocked by the things Jesus did and said right after his temptation.

Jesus came to Galilee and started to preach everywhere he went. He called everyone to repent because the Kingdom of heaven was at hand. I had no idea what he meant by the Kingdom, but my interest was piqued. Then he recruited four fishermen to follow him and become fishers of men instead. Jesus continued to preach and heal people from all kinds of diseases, and soon huge crowds were following him.

That's when he climbed the mountain, sat down, and began to teach his followers so they could grasp what he was doing and why. The heading was "Sermon on the Mount."

Here is what Jesus said:[15]

Blessed are the poor in spirit: for theirs is the kingdom of heaven.
Blessed are they that mourn: for they shall be comforted.
Blessed are the meek: for they shall inherit the earth.
Blessed are they which do hunger and thirst after righteousness:
for they shall be filled.
Blessed are the merciful: for they shall obtain mercy.
Blessed are the pure in heart: for they shall see God.
Blessed are the peacemakers: for they shall be called the children of God.
Blessed are they which are persecuted for righteousness' sake: for theirs is the
kingdom.

I knew I needed blessing. I needed help. I needed to change.

As I scanned the eight types of people who Jesus said were blessed, I knew immediately that I had nothing in common with the last six types of people. The meek in my book were the losers who did not stand up for their ideas. Not me!

What came to mind with the people hungering and thirsting for righteousness was a picture of striking workers asking for fair

---

[15] Matthew 5:3-10, KJV

wages, protest marchers asking for justice, or the lone Chinese student standing in front of a tank in Tiananmen Square.

Not me for sure.

The merciful were the people who empathized with others and extended forgiveness for failures and shortcomings. The closest I came to that was giving a poor performer six months to clean up mistakes and straighten out her performance.

The pure in heart brought great conviction. My heart was filled with self, success, sex, food, drink, work issues, work issues, and more work issues. The closest I came to pure in heart was Marianne and her constant love, care, and attention.

Peacemakers were diplomats, negotiators, and masters of compromise. That was for the United Nations and Bill Clinton. The Oslo accords just signed between the Israelis and Palestinians came to mind. That was not me.

It would be ludicrous to think I was being persecuted because I was righteous. I was far from righteous. I wasn't exactly sure what the term meant, but I knew that it wasn't me.

This was discouraging. It did not help my guilty heart.

But I might be a fit for number two. I was mourning. I was mourning my situation and the losses I had experienced. I was mourning my failures in marriage, family, and the impossible demands of work. It would be good to be comforted, but again I never let anyone get close enough to me to really experience that.

I marked myself as a maybe.

Finally, I came back to number one—the poor in spirit. What did that mean? If it meant people who were down on life, then that was me. Could it be? What if it meant people who were spiritually poor? I qualified for that. You might say I was a spiritual zero. I had never examined my spiritual life.

That was a clear signpost.

As we began our descent into Hong Kong, I put the New Testament back into my briefcase and something dawned on me. Jesus was reading my mail; it was like he was speaking to me! He was reaching into my confused and troubled heart with piercing words that helped me see my situation without shame.

He was blessing all kinds of people, even "spiritual zeros".

I felt like I was in a tractor beam. The Kingdom of heaven was opening to me. It was a crystal-clear signpost and a whole new way of thinking.

Then something unexpected happened. A moment of clarity emerged in my troubled brain. It was time to tell my management that I was unable to continue in my current assignment. I was pushing the nuclear button on my career. Waving a white flag was not the P&G way.

My pride had to be put aside. I somehow trusted that the consequences to my career and financial security would be tolerable. P&G would likely send me back to Canada. Worst case, I would find a job with another company. I knew this would be better for my kids. I knew this would be better for Marianne, and for me.

A clear first step to finding a better way.

The conversation with Marianne was marked by relief. She felt the way I did and knew me well enough to know that something had to give. She was reassuring, calm, confident in the future, and totally at peace. Her patience and joy were remarkable. She made me feel like I had faced the situation and come to the right next step.

I spoke to Dimitri the next time I saw him. He reacted with care and with authenticity. He knew I was not in the best place with the travel and workload.

The next person I talked to was AG, and the conversation went much the same way. I was unsure what would be next, but I could work with a clear mind.

I was setting healthy boundaries for the first time.

The process of being brutally honest with my life helped me clarify my priorities. I began to take the train into Guangzhou Monday mornings and to come home Thursday nights, working Fridays in the Hong Kong office. These simple changes brought much-needed thinking space.

I spent more time with Marianne and the kids. It was so refreshing. We went on junk boat rides in the harbor, hikes in the hills, and bike rides, and I even made some of the kids' school events. We tried new restaurants downtown and continued to enjoy our special date nights at our favorite seafood restaurant in Sheko.

Our Sundays were the one predictable thing throughout our time in Hong Kong. We got up and ate bacon and pancakes, then headed down to church in the mid-levels section of the City. Hong Kong Union was a mix of several protestant denominations and offered an English-speaking worship service for people from many countries and traditions. After church, we ate then spent the day at a beach, hiking, or bike riding.

I grew up Catholic and left the church when I went to college. Marianne grew up Protestant and was much more engaged in her faith than I was. We were married at St Andrews United

Church in Comber, Ontario—her hometown. We attended her church of choice everywhere we lived.

Surprisingly, I was quite regular in attending worship services on Sunday mornings throughout our marriage. Marianne was the driver, but I joined in. We both felt it was a good rhythm for our children. I may have been hung over at times, but I found nuggets in the sermons.

In some strange way, I was being drawn.

One Sunday in the new year, our church announced that there would be a special three-day retreat for men in mid-March and one for women the following week. I experienced another moment of clarity and knew instantly that I needed to attend that retreat.

That tractor beam again.

The idea of a three-day retreat to a beautiful place in northern Hong Kong sounded like just what I needed, and Marianne felt the same way.

When we got home, I checked my rolling 90-day calendar posted on the wall in my study. It contained all my travel and meeting commitments so Marianne could know where I was and how to reach me. The calendar was jampacked for 90 days—all except the Thursday afternoon to Sunday afternoon of March 14-17, 1996, which were totally open.

I had never been on a retreat. They said it would be a life-changing time of learning and growth. I signed up with great expectations of walks in the woods, the occasional lecture, good food, and plenty of time to rest and think. I was expectant.

Reflection question:

Think of a time when a "signpost event" led to a significant new insight.

Practical application:

What changes are most needed in your life right now?

(Don't wait for an earthquake!)

My internal gridlock was breaking up.

I could feel something big on the way.

Chapter 5

Treasure: Discovering True Purpose.

"For well thou know'st to my dear doting heart,
Thou art the fairest and most precious jewel."

~ Shakespeare

"He is no fool who gives up what he cannot keep
to gain what he cannot lose."

~ Jim Elliot

On a sunny Thursday afternoon in mid-March, I took a taxi to Sha Tin, north of Kowloon. The taxi pulled up to the Tao Fong Shan Retreat Center, which looked like a Buddhist monastery. I was exhausted but really looking forward to the weekend.

As I came through the front door, a few guys were welcoming the guests. One took my roller luggage and escorted me to my room. It was a comfortable college-style room, with a large window, a single bed, a desk with a chair, and a clean bathroom. I was one of the early arrivals, so I went out to explore the place a bit.

The campus had several pagoda-style buildings. Ornate rock gardens framed carefully trimmed trees, and fountains gurgled quietly. An outdoor meditation shelter led to a path through the bamboo forest that featured more benches for meditation. There were a few paths like it so people could spread out and be alone. The place was peaceful.

By dinner time, the 48 men on the guest list had arrived. We had a simple meal followed by introductions of the retreat team and instructions for the weekend.

We were told to take off our watches and put them in our luggage until Sunday. We were asked to make name tags and only use our first names all weekend, not divulging what we did for work. Here, we would simply be brothers. We were organized into 8 tables of 6 men, and two men from the retreat team joined each table group.

The format of the weekend was simple. There would be five short talks every day, followed by discussion and an activity. Three square meals. Quiet and rest between 10 p.m. and 6 a.m. daily. The set-up was straightforward and friendly. We all headed to bed for a good night's rest.

The first talk on Friday morning was about priorities. It was presented by a guy who was a successful surgeon. He was totally wrapped up in his work, he was an absentee dad, and his marriage was on the rocks.

One day, he got a call that his oldest son had been in a serious car wreck. His heart was pierced and everything he held dear became suddenly worthless. He left the operating room and rushed to be by his son's side.

In tears, he told us about the futility of what he was chasing. He stopped working for several weeks to be at his son's side. Through the process of his son's healing, he re-ordered his priorities. He asked his wife and kids to forgive him and altered his schedule.

I felt like the entire talk was a direct message for me.

My face was hot and flushed.

It was the first time I had seen a guy confess his mistakes and failures in front of other men. He spoke bluntly. I was shaken by the similarity of his story to mine.

I knew my own marriage would be in trouble if Marianne knew everything. I knew my kids were far away emotionally.

I felt like my decision to ask for a job change was in the nick of time. I cried at my stupidity. Yet I began to feel hopeful as I heard about this guy taking steps to reset his priorities.

The weekend continued with the same kind of raw honesty from each guy who spoke. I wasn't the only guy crying either. Many guys were cut to the heart. As the weekend went on, it always felt like each speaker was addressing me personally.

The tractor beam of conviction enveloped me.

At other times, I cried and released pent-up emotions that had their origins in my broken family and my own traumas.

Each time I felt hope, as the men speaking shared the specific ways Jesus had brought them peace, purpose, and significance.

This was another first for me—hearing men speaking about Jesus in a personal, practical, and non-religious way. The formality of my spiritual experiences in school and church had caused me to see God as a distant and nebulous person.

In my mind, Jesus was a great man and teacher. But without much exposure to the Bible, I knew little about him. I was intrigued with the bits I had recently read, but still didn't have much to go on.

What was happening in the retreat added considerably to my meager understanding. Each guy who spoke shared Bible passages about the Kingdom and how Jesus had changed their lives.

I learned that the Kingdom of Jesus was at work throughout the world today, to bring a new way of living through people who love and follow him. There was a mysterious quality to the Kingdom. I felt the spiritual tractor beam again.

I was being drawn into this amazing new world.

I wondered if the Kingdom was at work in Marianne to bring about the change I was seeing in her. I wondered if God used the earthquake to get my attention. Was the sudden clarity about leaving my assignment in China a Kingdom directive?

In each man's story, their moment of reckoning brought them to see that they were living in ignorance or opposition to God. Their stories were unique, but the pattern was similar. They came to a place of knowing that what they were doing was wrong, opposed to God, refusing to let him be the Boss.

It was exactly what I felt.

I was an enemy of the Kingdom, and I felt the brokenness of a life that was opposed to God. Disobeying the way God designed me to live had left me empty and guilty.

How could I address my guilt? The other speakers answered my questions as if God were reading my mind.

One speaker talked about the identity of Jesus and his purposes. I was blown away to hear that Jesus is called the Word of God, and that he is fully God, equal to God his Father. Jesus is the Creator. And Jesus is also fully human, one of us, among us and for us. John writes:

In the beginning the Word already existed. The Word was with God, and the Word was God. He existed in the beginning with God. God created everything through him, and nothing was created except through him. The Word gave life to everything that was created, and his life brought light to everyone. ... The Word became human and made his home among us.[16]

---

[16] John 1:1-4, 14, NLT. This is one of the Bible's most important descriptions of Jesus, and a key focus of the "The Walk to Emmaus" retreat. See upperroom.org/walktoemmaus.

He shared God's motive of love in sending Jesus:

For this is how God loved the world: He gave his one and only Son, so that everyone who believes in him will not perish but have eternal life.

God sent his Son into the world not to judge the world, but to save the world through him.[17]

The idea of God the Father giving his only son Jesus up to death struck a chord. It was an act of love. The speaker also shared the process by which people experience eternal Kingdom life:

I assure you, no one can enter the Kingdom of God without being born of water and the Spirit. Humans can reproduce only human life, but the Holy Spirit gives birth to spiritual life.

So don't be surprised when I say, 'You must be born again.'[18]

I knew I needed a spiritual life. I needed a new life too.

Another speaker talked about the reality of wrongdoing by every human being, which the Bible calls sin, and the punishment required for this sin against an eternal and holy God:

All people are under the power of sin. As the Scriptures say, No one is righteous—not even one. No one is truly wise; no one is seeking God.

All have turned away; all have become useless. No one does good, not a single one. For no one can ever be made right with God by doing what the law commands.

The law simply shows us how sinful we are.
You are now ashamed of the things you used to do, things that end in eternal doom. For the wages of sin is death.[19]

---

[17] John 3:16-17, NLT
[18] John 3:5-7, NIV
[19] Romans 3:9-12, 20, 6:21-23, NLT

He showed us the way that God could forgive our sins and yet maintain his perfect standard - by punishing Jesus instead!

Yet God, in his grace, freely makes us right in his sight. He did this through Christ Jesus when he freed us from the penalty for our sins. For God presented Jesus as the sacrifice for sin. People are made right with God when they believe that Jesus sacrificed his life, shedding his blood.[20]

Yet another speaker shared how the sacrificial death of Jesus can be received by those who want the Kingdom and a relationship with Jesus, by believing, accepting, and being born again:

But to all who believed him and accepted him, he gave the right to become children of God. They are reborn—not with a physical birth resulting from human passion or plan, but a birth that comes from God.[21]

He explained that our sin is forgiven not because we work extra hard to balance our "good and bad deed scales" or by doing penance, community service, attending church, and giving money. Our sin is forgiven by the grace of God through faith in Jesus:

God saved you by his grace when you believed. And you can't take credit for this; it is a gift from God. Salvation is not a reward for the good things we have done, so none of us can boast about it.[22]

It is only the death of Jesus that covers our misdeeds and brings us into his Kingdom:

The Father has qualified you to share in the inheritance of his holy people in the kingdom of light. For he has rescued us from the dominion of darkness and brought us into the kingdom of the Son he loves, in whom we have redemption, the forgiveness of sins.[23]

---

[20] Romans 3:24-25, NLT
[21] John 1:12-13, NLT
[22] Ephesians 2:8-9, NLT
[23] Colossians 1:13-14, NIV

Another guy shared the process of pledging allegiance to Jesus:

If you openly declare that Jesus is Lord and believe in your heart that God raised him from the dead, you will be saved. For it is by believing in your heart that you are made right with God, and it is by openly declaring your faith that you are saved.[24]

By the time these guys finished sharing their mistakes and the pain they had caused others, I was in tears.

I understood the guilt I felt for the first time. I was guilty of opposing God. I knew it. But I also hated what I had done and began to turn toward God, leaving my selfish ways.

At the same time, I felt an incredible relief. The ugly weight of my sin had been covered by Jesus. I had never grasped this message in all my years of Catholic churches and schools and all my years in Protestant churches. I was stunned.

What I now understood—for the first time—was the biggest idea I had ever heard.

The Creator of the universe loved me! God the Father, God the Son, and God the Holy Spirit had collaborated in love to bring the Kingdom of redemption into their creation, and I could be included - simply by faith!

God's Kingdom tractor beam was on me.

I was exploding with unbridled relief and happiness.

I felt like Liam Neeson's daughter at the end of the movie *Taken*. Her bloody, injured father, the one she avoided and ridiculed her whole life, had given everything to rescue her. Her foolish and careless pursuit of trivial pleasures despite his warnings had dragged her into a future of slavery and death. Despite her

---

[24] Romans 10:9-10, NLT

rejection he bravely, intelligently, and skillfully gave all he had, risking death to set her free.

Jesus had done that for me on the bloody cross.

I saw Jesus in a new light. He had left the perfection of heaven to become one of us and teach us the way to live. He walked his talk. He was brilliant, witty, fearless, and faithful.

Despite opposition and ridicule, he stood firm, always gracious and full of truth. At the point of his tortuous death, he forgave his killers. He rose from the grave to defeat death. He's opened his Kingdom to all who will leave their selfish ways. His offer stands regardless of who we are or what we have done.

How can you not love and pledge allegiance to a King like that?

I was not too far gone.
I had a way out.
I had hope.
I had eternal life.
I had treasure.
I had the Kingdom.
I had Jesus.
My hard heart was conquered by love.
I had the biggest idea ever.
I had found my true purpose.

That night I went for a hike. The wind rustled through the creaking bamboo. I came to the peak, and there was a huge cross lit with spotlights. I stood under the cross and asked Jesus to make real what I had just glimpsed for the first time.

At that moment the wind stopped, and everything grew quiet. I felt the presence of Jesus. I had never experienced that kind of love and peace and joy.

I felt him reaching inside my chest and pulling out what felt like a 60-pound rock. This was the weight of my sin and my hard heart, and he placed it at the foot of the cross.

I felt light and free. It was all so real.

I was loved, accepted, and forgiven. My spirit soared. I stood there for what felt like hours, with thankful tears of joy.

I needed to talk about what happened. I asked the organizers if there was a Catholic priest available. Somehow, I felt a strong need to confess all my sins. The last time I had done a confession was with a priest in high school.

When Elmer came around the corner, I was dumbfounded. He was one of the 48 guys in the retreat. He was in his mid-sixties and had a mane of thick white hair. He wore a golf shirt from Pebble Beach Golf Club. He looked like an executive.

Confused, I said, "Elmer, what's a priest doing with so many fancy golf shirts?" He said, "Oh, an executive in my congregation just died, and his widow gave me his shirts."

I asked, "Would you please take my confession?". He said, "Sure." He prayed then asked me how long it had been. When I said 22 years, he just smiled and asked me to go on. He had amazing warmth, acceptance, and never flinched.

He'd heard it all before.

I went on for about two hours. I started with what happened on the mountain and told him my life would never be the same again now that Jesus had picked me out of the pit.

He listened, asked for clarification on a few items, and patiently attended to me as I poured out my heart. At some point, I must have begun repeating myself, so he gently held up his hand and said, "Denis, I think we are done".

He pronounced my sins forgiven with this amazing promise from the Bible as he prayed:

If we confess our sins, he is faithful and just and will forgive us our sins and purify us from all unrighteousness.[25]

Then he said, "Let me give you one piece of advice". I was all ears. He said, "Denis, you are a hard charging leader, but Jesus is the Boss now. Stay out of his way. Listen to him!" It felt like the counsel of a loving father.

His warm presence reminded me of the "father gap" in my life. Being with Elmer was like having a new father—someone wise, gentle, and yet firm, who genuinely cared about me.

Elmer pointed me to my Father in heaven.

When I started my relationship with Jesus, I was reunited with my true Father. He would never let me down. Because of Jesus, I was adopted into the family of God, part of the family business, written into his will.

I had found my true self and true purpose.

I left Elmer elated, free, and light. I was so thankful for his counsel. The mirage of material wealth evaporated, and I had a heart filled with the glow of God's fiery love. Grace—the undeserved favor of God—had been poured out on me.

I'd never be the same again.

This love and grace surprised me. It was what I had been chasing my whole life. I finally saw the kingdom because I was finally

---

[25] 1 John 1:9, NIV

able to see my need. The kingdom was for those who admitted their spiritual poverty.

As the retreat ended on Sunday afternoon, we were given a chance to share our experience. I wasn't the only one Jesus touched. The stories from other men blew me away.

We had been visited by the King.

Marianne had some inkling of what was going on, because in my last two nightly check-in calls, I was in tears and telling her I had never experienced anything like this retreat. On Sunday afternoon, she heard me share what God had done. I don't recall exactly what I said, but it was something like, "I am changed forever, my life will never be the same. I belong to Jesus."

Over the next few days, Marianne knew she had a new husband. And I finally understood all the changes happening in Marianne's life. I was so excited. I asked her why she hadn't shared the Good News with me before. She replied: "Are you kidding? That would have taken forever. Only God could get through to you."

I found out that the organizers had hundreds of people praying for us by name. Marianne had her entire spiritual community praying for me. The power of God had been released and prayers had been answered. Jesus' Sermon on the Mount was coming to life in me.

The man who was mourning had been comforted. The man so poor in spirit had received the Kingdom of heaven. I finally knew what it was to be blessed.

Jesus had been true to his words.

Now I needed to unpack this amazing blessing. I wanted to learn more about what had happened to me, and how to pursue my new purpose.

I had begun a journey with Jesus who is called "The Word." Every guy who spoke that weekend talked about the beauty and necessity of knowing the Jesus of the Bible. Without that, all we have is personal creeds with moral odds and ends thrown in - a god created by us to suit us.

I did not have a Bible in a modern translation, but a good friend started me on the right path. Bill heard about my experience over the weekend and came by to tell me that he had begun his journey with Jesus just a few months before me.

What are the odds that Jesus would sign up another P&G Vice President in Hong Kong just months apart? Bill and I had worked together as we shared different assignments in Asia over a period of several years. After leaving P&G, Bill was leading the Asia business of another company. We stayed in contact and played golf occasionally.

He gave me a beautiful leather study Bible, a devotional book, and a CD of powerful worship songs. He encouraged me to start each day with praise and worship. Then read the Word, meditate on it, and put it into practice. As I woke up each day, I could not wait to meet with Jesus.

The King was alive in me. The Kingdom was coming.

The Biggest Idea Ever had dawned in my life.

Reflection question:

Have you ever felt like God was coming after you?

Practical application:

How are you responding to the Good News of Jesus?

I wanted to know more.

God was ready to oblige with a really good book.

Chapter 6

Logos: Hear God's Voice, Defeat Anxiety.

"The Bible is the most influential book in all of history.
God's word impacts society in many ways,
some of which we are yet to comprehend."

~ Dr. Jordan B. Peterson

"A thorough knowledge of the Bible
is worth more than a college education".

~ Theodore Roosevelt

Logos is Greek for "the word." In Greek philosophy, *Logos* refers to divine reason or the power that puts sense into the world to make order instead of chaos. It is the idea of a word uttered by a living voice that embodies a concept or teaches truth. A tour guide in Greece once told me that *Logos* also implies a very big idea.

One of Jesus' nicknames is Logos.

He is "The Word." He speaks and things happen. His voice was central in creation and in the writing of the Bible. Because he is the living word offering profound teaching and the biggest ideas, the Bible is the first and best place to know Jesus.

The Bible feeds my relationship with Jesus and my understanding of the Kingdom. My highest hope is that my story will inspire you to begin a Logos journey of your own.

I vividly remember the days following the retreat. I woke up at 5 a.m. so I could have a couple of hours alone with God. I loved the quiet time before dawn, listening, enjoying his presence, starting the day slowly.

The time was so good that I began going to bed early!

I started with a single Bible verse and let it soak in as I meditated and worshiped. I pondered the lyrics of the worship songs as I focused my heart and mind on Jesus.

I listened in silence, asking him to speak. During the retreat, we were given journals and the leaders encouraged us to write down what we felt God was saying. I slowly learned to hear my true Dad's voice as I absorbed the unfolding Scriptural story.

I wrote down whatever thoughts came to mind. Sometimes it was encouragement, like, "Denis, I love spending time with you." Or it might be a correction, like, "Denis, you need to apologize for the way you spoke to Marianne yesterday."

Of course, there were times of distraction, like remembering to prepare for a meeting, or call the plumber, or wondering where I left my checkbook. I simply jotted those down and returned to my posture of listening.

Over time, I grew in my ability to concentrate, meditate, and listen quietly. I experienced a whole new sense of peace, getting centered and grounded in God's presence, his written Word, and his gentle promptings.

My constant vigilance and anxiety over life's challenges slowly disappeared. Peace ruled over me. I realized that meditating on God's Word and enjoying his presence is a powerful antidote to anxiety! Hearing God is one of his thrilling promises to us all:

Call to me and I will answer you and tell you great and unsearchable things you do not know.[26]

---

[26] Jeremiah 33:3 NIV

I had read about the effects of meditation in corporate effectiveness and taken some training in meditation techniques, but I was never able to make it stick. The big difference for me was that I was now meeting with someone very special who had awesome content.

This time helped me build my relationship with God and grew to impact my marriage, my parenting, my friendships, and most surprisingly, my work. It was amazing how often the Bible spoke practically into my daily work issues.

I asked God about the day's meetings and priorities at work along with my personal and family priorities. I learned to pray for everyone in my family and ask God how I could bless them. I prayed for each person on my work schedule, as well as key decisions. I asked for wisdom and creativity and Jesus granted it!

I became less anxious, more resilient, less hurried, and more thoughtful. I set better priorities. I developed better relationships. I often received new ideas from God.

To be clear, this was a journey. I still missed opportunities to listen and treated people improperly. But I had a new habit that added great value to my life.

What is so special about the Bible?

In this chapter, I want to share what I discovered. I recognize this chapter will raise many questions – they are questions many of us have. I won't have time to cover them in detail, but I will offer some resources I find helpful.

Did you know that the Bible is the perennial global best seller? Sadly, only one in five Americans has read it through.[27]

---

[27] https://aleteia.org/2017/05/15/the-bible-is-widely-owned-but-not-well-known-new-study-finds/

The Bible has outlasted kingdoms and civilizations. It stands alone as the central story in human civilization and has been the key to literature of all kinds for centuries. It has spawned classic novels, theater, poetry, music, and films.

Yet, it is not really a book. It is more like a library, holding 66 books and letters that were written over a period of 1,500 years by more than 40 authors who came from all walks of life.

The Old Testament was written between 1400 BC and 400 BC, mostly in Hebrew with some sections in Aramaic. It is grouped in three parts—the Law, the Prophets, and the Writings. By combining the first Hebrew syllables for each of these three parts, we get the word "Tanakh." That's still how Jews refer to their Bible.

The New Testament was written in Greek over the last half of the first century, by the Jewish disciples of Jesus or by those they influenced. The New Testament is also in three parts. The four eyewitness biographies of Jesus are called Gospels. The book of Acts and the letters by the disciples of Jesus describe the early church and expand on the teaching of Jesus. Revelation is a prophecy of the return of Jesus and the new creation.

Other texts, called the Apocrypha, written in the period between the Old and the New Testaments, can be found in some Bible translations. These are helpful but they are not considered as authoritative as the others.

Obviously, most of us will not read the original texts.

We depend on the scholars who have produced translations into hundreds of languages. English speakers have dozens of translations to choose from. I recommend using modern translations like the English Standard Version, the New

International Version, or the New Living Translation. They vary in translation approach and comparing them is helpful.

When you read the Bible, you are reading the very words of God! Every word is God-given and written down by the prophetic authors as they were led by the Holy Spirit:

All Scripture is inspired by God and is useful to teach us what is true and to make us realize what is wrong in our lives. It corrects us when we are wrong and teaches us to do what is right. God uses it to prepare and equip his people to do every good work.[28]

No prophecy of Scripture comes from someone's own interpretation. For no prophecy was ever produced by the will of man, but men spoke from God as they were carried along by the Holy Spirit.[29]

Jesus says that the Old Testament Scriptures are about him too: *"And beginning with Moses and all the Prophets, he explained to them what was said in all the Scriptures concerning himself."*[30]

How can the Bible's ancient books be relevant today?

True, the Bible presents challenges in interpretation, even though much of it is easy to understand. We do need to know the context for each book and where it fits in world history.

This is where a good study Bible comes in, with charts, notes, explanations for the more difficult passages, and an index of topics and keywords to help find what you need.

Here are examples of the Bible's ongoing relevance - imagine if everyone you knew practiced the wisdom contained in these four simple verses:

---

[28] 2 Timothy 3:16-17, NLT
[29] 2 Peter 1:20-21, ESV
[30] Luke 24:27, NIV

- *So whatever you wish that others would do to you, do also to them.*

- *Let every person be quick to hear, slow to speak, slow to anger.*

- *And whenever you stand praying, forgive, if you have anything against anyone, so that your Father also who is in heaven may forgive you your trespasses.*

- *Don't agree to guarantee another person's debt.*[31]

The Word of God sizzles with divine presence, life, and power. You can read a passage for the tenth time, and it might land on you with unexpected clarity, conviction, and relevance for the first time. It's the only book that promises to read you:

For the word of God is living and active, sharper than any two-edged sword, piercing to the division of soul and of spirit, of joints and of marrow, and discerning the thoughts and intentions of the heart.[32]

No other book gives so much detail about God and his ways:

His name: *Then Moses said to God, "If I come to the people of Israel and say to them, 'The God of your fathers has sent me to you,' and they ask me, 'What is his name?' what shall I say to them?" God said to Moses, "I am who I am." And he said, "Say this to the people of Israel: 'I am has sent me to you.'*[33]

His character: *And he passed in front of Moses, proclaiming, "The Lord, the Lord, the compassionate and gracious God, slow to anger, abounding in love and faithfulness."*[34]

His son: *And when Jesus was baptized, immediately he went up from the water, and behold, the heavens were opened to him, and he saw the Spirit of*

---

[31] Matthew 7:12, James 1:19, Matthew 11:25, Proverbs 22:26, NLT
[32] Hebrews 4:12, ESV
[33] Exodus 3:14-15, ESV
[34] Exodus 34:6, ESV

God descending like a dove and coming to rest on him; and behold, a voice from heaven said, "This is my beloved Son, with whom I am well pleased." [35]

His plan: *God has now revealed to us his mysterious plan regarding Christ, a plan to fulfill his own good pleasure. And this is the plan: At the right time he will bring everything together under the authority of Christ— everything in heaven and on earth.* [36]

Jesus and his Kingdom: *As my vision continued that night, I saw someone like a son of man coming with the clouds of heaven. He approached the Ancient One and was led into his presence. He was given authority, honor, and sovereignty over all the nations of the world, so that people of every race and nation and language would obey him. His rule is eternal— it will never end. His kingdom will never be destroyed.* [37]

Jesus and his humble invitation: *Come to me, all you who are weary and burdened, and I will give you rest. Take my yoke upon you and learn from me, for I am gentle and humble in heart, and you will find rest for your souls. For my yoke is easy and my burden is light.* [38]

My time with the Father reading his Word together has brought such good fruit. My early days studying Matthew's Gospel were life changing.

Something huge had happened to me at the retreat - I was on fire. Marianne warned me that I couldn't expect everyone to be excited about Jesus. After all, I had been in church a lot and didn't have the lights come on until I was 38 years old. Jesus spoke so practically to me every morning:

"Blessed are you when people insult you, persecute you and falsely say all kinds of evil against you because of me. Rejoice and be glad, because great is your reward in heaven, for in the same way they persecuted the prophets who

---

[35] Matthew 3:16-17, ESV
[36] Ephesians 1:9-10, NLT
[37] Daniel 7:13-14, NLT
[38] Matthew 11:28-30, NIV

were before you. You are the salt of the earth. But if the salt loses its saltiness, how can it be made salty again? It is no longer good for anything, except to be thrown out and trampled underfoot. You are the light of the world. A town built on a hill cannot be hidden. Neither do people light a lamp and put it under a bowl. Instead, they put it on its stand, and it gives light to everyone in the house. In the same way, let your light shine before others, that they may see your good deeds and glorify your Father in heaven." [39]

Jesus was warning me to be ready for some negative responses when talking about him. Don't let others' reactions steal your joy. Just be salt and light. Salt is a preservative and flavor enhancer, so let your actions preserve goodwill and enhance relationships by serving people well. Let the change in your life exude joy and be an influence for good.

I had broken relationships at work due to my self-centeredness, pride, and impatience. Jesus spoke directly to me:

"You have heard that it was said to the people long ago, "You shall not murder, and anyone who murders will be subject to judgment." But I tell you that anyone who is angry with a brother or sister will be subject to judgment. Again, anyone who says to a brother or sister, "Raca," is answerable to the court. And anyone who says, "You fool!" will be in danger of the fire of hell. "Therefore, if you are offering your gift at the altar and there remember that your brother or sister has something against you, leave your gift there in front of the altar. First go and be reconciled to them; then come and offer your gift." [40]

Jesus was telling me to hold my Sunday offering, and first address the people who have something legitimate against me. He made it a high priority to meet with those people, repent of bad behavior, ask forgiveness, and reconcile.

---

[39] Matthew 5:11-16, NIV
[40] Matthew 5:21-24, NIV

Jesus raised the bar on my anger and pointed out that unchecked anger was the pathway to murder. I hadn't murdered anyone, but I had attacked some coworkers with blistering critiques of their value. (The word *raca* above means "good for nothing.")

I had labeled an HR manager that way (under my breath) and went to him and asked forgiveness for my rude and impatient behavior. I met with five or six people in the first few weeks, confessing anger, gossip, slander, impatience, and pride.

Did that ever change my work team dynamics!

I came into the Kingdom with a stinging conscience regarding my lack of sexual purity. I wasn't sure exactly what to do, but this passage encouraged me and started me in the right direction:

You have heard that it was said, "You shall not commit adultery." But I tell you that anyone who looks at a woman lustfully has already committed adultery with her in his heart. If your right eye causes you to stumble, gouge it out and throw it away. It is better for you to lose one part of your body than for your whole body to be thrown into hell. And if your right hand causes you to stumble, cut it off and throw it away. It is better for you to lose one part of your body than for your whole body to go into hell. [41]

That hit me like a ton of bricks. Jesus set a high bar for sexual purity, focusing on my eyes, imagination, and inner thoughts. The study notes clarified that Jesus wasn't advocating self-mutilation, but rather the immediate abandonment of sin habits that could lead to spiritual ruin.

I also looked up purity and found this verse:

How can a young person stay on the path of purity? By living according to your word.

I seek you with all my heart; do not let me stray from your commands.

---

[41] Matthew 5:27-30, NIV

I have hidden your word in my heart that I might not sin against you.[42]

I asked God to help me memorize Scripture and say no to pornography and illicit sex. As I listened, I heard, "No sexual pleasure unless present with Marianne." It came in a firm, fatherly voice without condemnation. It was an otherworldly phrase, certainly nothing I made up. When I was alone, I remembered that mantra. I carried pictures of Marianne and my kids when I was on the road to help me stay focused and pure.

It wasn't easy, but God was faithful to set me free from that destructive sexual addiction. I'm still free three decades later.

Having been an absentee dad, I needed to address my parenting. I began reading the book of Proverbs, one chapter a day. It is a compendium of pithy sayings that provide brilliant insights to marriage, sex, fatherhood, motherhood, parenting, work, finances, and relationships. In the first chapter, this rang my bell:

The fear of the Lord is the beginning of knowledge, but fools despise wisdom and instruction.

Listen, my son, to your father's instruction and do not forsake your mother's teaching.[43]

I had been parenting without knowing the Lord, or without being in awe of him. I was short on knowledge and wisdom, and unlike Marianne, had been doing very little instruction of my kids. Disciplining a child without first training them only leads to frustration.

My schedule was creating inconsistency in their worlds.

I confessed my absence and asked for their forgiveness. I started to read books with them while seeking wisdom from God. I

[42] Psalm 119:9-11, NIV
[43] Proverbs 1:7-8, NIV

realized that my oldest son Denis, at the time almost 11 years old, would be going to college in 350 weeks. That really challenged me to develop a father's instruction plan. Later in their teen years, I trained them in the wisdom of the Proverbs.

Mornings with God were so life-giving. I felt like a garden being fertilized, weeded, watered, and bathed in the sun. I was sprouting with new growth and fruit, while God also pruned my life's dead branches away and pulled out weeds of anger, addiction, and broken relationships. I was a work in progress.

But nothing like this would have happened without the discipline of being in the Word of God, listening, asking, praying, seeking. I routinely ask God for direction, and he routinely grants wisdom and understanding, just as he promised![44]

It's impossible to exaggerate the impact of discovering God for yourself by studying the Scriptures with an open heart.

My first time reading through the Bible changed my life. I experienced the love and patience of God in a radical new way. I saw human nature captured so clearly.

I saw myself so clearly in God's story.

The Bible opened my mind on so many subjects. I was learning about love, sacrifice, relationships, work, and the future.

The Kingdom of God is a massive idea - the biggest ever - a sparkling vision of a better world filled with eternal hope.

A few years ago, I visited the Museum of the Bible in Washington D.C.[45] The museum was conceived and generously funded by the Green family, owners of Hobby Lobby.

---

[44] See John 10:27
[45] See museumofthebible.org, and check out *This Beautiful Book*, by Steve Green.

75

The giant brass entry gates of the museum contain the reverse text of the book of Genesis in Latin, as set by Gutenberg on the first movable-type press. That technology enabled access to the Bible for all believers in their own language, revealing heresy practiced by the church and spawning the Reformation.

The exhibits beautifully capture the beauty of the Bible, the preservation of the Bible through the centuries, and the influence of the Bible on all domains of human flourishing.

The museum displays the efforts to translate the Bible into every language, and how the YouVersion app brings the Bible through the Internet to ordinary people all over the earth today.

I became convinced that it is simply not possible to be well educated without knowing the Bible. If this book does nothing except cause you to read the Bible with an open heart, it will have been totally worthwhile.

Don't rely on others' opinions, discover what it says for yourself.

Only the Bible claims to be the unchanging Word of God. Only the Bible contains the answers to our origins. One of Stephen Hawking's contributions to scientific knowledge, corroborated by others, is that our universe had a beginning. Of course, that discovery still leaves us with the question of the cause.

The Bible answers that clearly—a good God spoke it into existence. Only the Bible has a perfect record on prophecy. The Bible predicted the birth, life, and death of Jesus in intricate detail. Only the Bible speaks to the heart and brings people to understand the transforming power of Jesus and his Spirit. The Bible is the key source for what Jesus taught and said about himself, and what will happen when he returns.

I realize this chapter is very challenging considering the pervasive efforts to discredit the Bible in academia. We have the theory of spontaneous life and random evolution, the famous failures of church leaders, and the examples of hypocrisy by Christians on a host of issues.

I acknowledge the legitimacy of these questions, I share them! The scope and focus of this book do not allow me to treat all these questions in detail. For these questions, I recommend two excellent resources.

The origins of life, the theory of evolution and the Bible's relationship with science have all shifted in the past 20 years. The latest advances in biology, chemistry, physics, and archaeology have confirmed the authority of the Bible. I recommend an insightful and entertaining book by my friend Eric Metaxas, a fantastic "one-stop" resource on these issues.[46]

Further, thorny questions about the impact of Christianity on the world have been made famous by those opposed to the faith. These charges include fostering violence, crushing diversity, denigrating women, condoning slavery, and fostering homophobic behavior.

Many wonder how an all-powerful and good God allows so much suffering on earth and eternal punishment in hell. These questions have been addressed thoughtfully and completely by many authors. I like the nuance and depth of a recent book written by Rebecca McLaughlin on these issues.[47]

I'll finish this chapter with a short story.

My best friend in high school was Tim Brac. We decided to attend Queen's University together, as Alex had written a letter of recommendation for him too. Tim was married between our junior and senior years to Marg, the love of his life.

---

[46] See *Is Atheism Dead?* by Eric Metaxas
[47] See *Confronting Christianity: 12 Hard Questions* by Rebecca McLaughlin

Tim was part of my wedding four years later. He went on to earn his Ph.D. in biology and became a consultant to governments. We stayed in touch over the years, and when he visited Cincinnati fifteen years ago, I gave him a copy of the Bible.

About eight years later, Tim opened that Bible and began reading it. After two trips through, Tim became convinced that Jesus was the true King and that his Kingdom was his only hope.

Over the last few years, we have enjoyed monthly phone calls together, where we share what we are learning and discuss what's going on in the world around us.

I am constantly stretched by Tim's careful thinking on a wide range of topics like global energy issues, food supply, biological warfare, synthetic virus creation, the philosophy of science, international tensions, and the application of Scripture.

Tim would say that he wasn't well educated until he became knowledgeable about the Bible. That requires both humility and a desire for the truth.

I urge you to commit to read it for yourself. May you hear God's voice, your true Dad's voice. May you understand yourself and the world better.

Most of all, may you experience peace instead of anxiety.

Reflection question:

What is holding you back from reading the Bible?

Practical application:

Go online and find a plan to read the Bible in one year. If that feels too daunting, start with the Gospel of John, the book of Proverbs and the letter to the Romans. Try the bibleproject.com website. They have videos explaining each book of the Bible.

The Bible opened my eyes to the stunning scope of God's plan for the world. It radically changed my daily experience of living, infusing me with vision and hope. Let's see why!

Chapter 7

Good News: Understanding the Biggest Idea Ever.

*"When God does what God intends to do,
this will be an act of fresh grace, and of radical newness."*

~ N.T. Wright

*"Seek first God's kingdom and what God wants.
Then all your other needs will be met as well."*

~ Jesus of Nazareth

My quality of life was being transformed. I experienced a newness, lightness, and freedom in my life. My relationships were growing in honesty and depth. My thinking was clear and sharp. I felt so alive.

My team's excitement over the upcoming launch of Crest in China was at a fever pitch. The National Committee for Oral Health gave Crest their endorsement. Our researchers had worked for years for this moment, and we celebrated them.

Our product formula scored huge wins in blind tests. Our R&D team had matched superior efficacy with excellent in-use aesthetics, and fantastic packaging.

Our advertising scored off the charts, with a powerful demo using an eggshell to show how Crest restored teeth and prevented decay. Research showed this advertising would change the category.

This supercharged work scenario unfolded as I was unpacking the Bible and learning about God's plan for the future of his world.

God's Kingdom plans went far beyond my best marketing plans.

Many churches completely ignore the most momentous things in the Bible. They present the idea of personal salvation and focus on the avoidance of hell. Eternity is rarely discussed, and usually features ephemeral notions about white gowns, blinding light, and disembodied spirits with harps in the clouds.

Some pastors say, "invite Jesus into your heart". Others plead with us to "accept Jesus as your personal savior". Others say, "just close your eyes and say this prayer." These are man-made sayings that are not in the Bible.

Worse, these statements shrink the message of Jesus. They reduce spiritual life to a transaction, keeping us firmly in control. This is the epitome of man-made religion. Rules, traditions, and untold efforts of people trying to find and please God.

These distortions can make us feel like spiritual orphans. Maybe you've seen a televangelist asking for money, or you were turned off by hypocritical religious people. Maybe you have been hurt by a church or frustrated with their political agendas.

The Kingdom of Jesus is so far beyond all that.

It is about a King who came to find us and save us.
Jesus is not groveling for acceptance, he's the boss!
He is not asking to be invited into our hearts.
He is calling us to change our thinking and follow him obediently.
He is warning us that we are in the wrong kingdom.
He is telling us that his Kingdom is the answer to all our needs.
He is announcing a new world order and his victory over evil.
He is inviting us to lose our life and make an exodus into his.
He did not come to start a new religion.
He came to launch his Kingdom.

His launch plan is the most strategic and creative I've ever seen.

Jesus dazzled me with the genius of his world-changing plan.

Let's start with the term *Good News*, which is also translated *Gospel*. This term was used in antiquity to describe a great military victory or the crowning of a new emperor. The emperor Augustus had a gospel message, announcing his victories and the Pax Romana.

Jesus repurposed this word deliberately. As the true Emperor of the universe, he announced that the long-awaited King and eternal Kingdom were finally here.

Jesus fulfilled Kingdom prophecies through his birth, death, resurrection, and ascension. And he made many more promises that he will fulfill when he returns to consummate his Kingdom.

As I learned more, my heart was set on fire by the sheer scope and beauty of his plan. His promises filled the deepest longings of my heart and the wildest hopes of my imagination.

I was rocked by what Isaiah said:

No eye has seen, no ear has heard, and no mind has imagined what God has prepared for those who love him.[48]

The Gospels clearly show Jesus saying he was God and proving it with miracles. His teaching and wisdom blew me away. He is the best leader I've ever seen, gladly giving his life for his followers. Jesus is the only one to rise from death, and the only one who promises to come back for us.

Everything I read about Jesus was pure and unique.

It's overwhelming. The Bible contains approximately 750 promises, usually spoken directly by God or delivered through his prophets. So far, about 600 of these have been fulfilled, many by the birth, life, ministry, death, and resurrection of Jesus.

---

[48] Isaiah 64:4

These are documented in many places, demonstrating the Bible's astounding reliability.[49]

When interviewing candidates at P&G, we had a saying that "the best indicator of future potential is past performance." Jesus has perfect past performance; you know he's going to deliver.

Of the approximately 150 biblical promises that remain to be fulfilled, about one third refer to the restoration of Israel. The existence of Israel since 1948 is a miracle of Bible prophecy unfolding on the global stage.

Jesus has kept his promises to Israel.

Examples include the rebirth of the nation, the resurrection of the Hebrew language, the return of huge numbers of Jews to Israel, the blessing of Israeli inventions for the world, the provision of water in the desert, and the protection of Israel against multiple enemies through miraculous military victories. Israel has been at the center of God's plan, it still is, and it will be. [50]

The remaining prophecies refer to the return of our Jewish Messiah and the advent of the new heavens and new earth. I will get to those amazing promises, but let's first look at the impact of Jesus and his Kingdom on our civilization so far:

- a global church (imperfect as it is) serving millions of people with love, food, shelter, and the hope of the good news.

- originators of great discoveries: Kepler, Copernicus, Newton, and Gutenberg to name just a few.

---

[49] For example, this list covers 55 prophecies: jesusfilm.org/blog/old-testament-prophecies/ many other lists are longer!
[50] The scope of this book prevents me from a deeper treatment of the miracle of Israel. The books in Appendix B will give you a start. You can also find an essay on Israel on my website: https://denisbeausejour.com/resources/

- founders of great universities such as Harvard, Yale, William & Mary, Queen's, and Notre Dame.

- practitioners of healing, medicine, and in most cities, the builders of the modern hospital.

- passionate sponsors of education, art, music, and literature.

- shapers of government ideals, the rule of law, and justice.

As good as that is, let's focus on the future. Our taste of the Kingdom now is just a small down payment on what is coming with the return of Jesus.

The more I read about the future promises in the Bible, the more excited I got. I discovered that the Bible promises answers to the most pressing and difficult problems we face today. I discovered that everything I always wanted is coming with Jesus:

1. **Global peace:** The threat of wars, famine, and economic collapse are an everyday part of life. We yearn for a global community that can function in peace and harmony. Jesus is going to bring lasting peace to his world.

2. **Medicine:** We are passionately seeking advances to deal with cancer, heart disease, auto-immune disorders, killers like multiple sclerosis and ALS, dementia, Alzheimer's, arthritis, obesity, diabetes, high blood pressure, strokes, infertility, and viruses. Jesus is going to bring a future of perfect physical well-being.

3. **Mental health:** Attention deficit, trauma, depression, anxiety, panic attacks, gender dysphoria, loneliness, suicide. A wave of mental health problems afflicts us. Jesus is going to bring a world where every person has a sound mind.

4. **Artificial Intelligence:** We hope one day that everyday tasks can be done safely by machines. We search for drugs that will enhance our human intelligence, memory, and imagination. Jesus will give us perfect clarity and wisdom.

5. **Aging:** We yearn for ways to turn back the clock, and new techniques that can change appearance and desirability: diet, drugs, plastic surgery, and gyms. We crave bodies that look young and healthy. We are still seeking the fountain of youth. Jesus is going to give us perfect bodies that never age.

6. **Environment:** We face climate change and the existential threat of a warming planet. Plastic waste invades the oceans. Fossil fuel exhaust threatens the air we breathe. Food and water problems abound. We desperately need new energy solutions. Jesus is going to provide limitless clean energy in a new cosmos of unlimited beauty, clean water, and fresh air in a spectacular garden city more wonderful than Eden.

7. **Spiritual connection:** Millions seek the experience of highest order tranquility, union with the divine, and connectivity with a higher power. Jesus will be with us for all eternity in a bond so intimate and enjoyable that marriage will no longer be necessary.

8. **Prosperity and justice:** So many live with poverty and injustice. We are looking for justice to be done and for all people to work, prosper and be treated with dignity. Jesus will usher in a just and sustainable economy filled with satisfying and creative work as we serve him.

9. **Relational thriving:** Families struggle with divorce, fatherlessness, and incarcerated parents. Communities face political division, racism, and violence. Jesus will live with us in the perfect love of a new human community.

10. **Meaning:** We want to make our lives count. We want to be fully known and fully loved, secure in our identity and destiny. Jesus will give us the experience of learning, creating, and serving forever. We will never exhaust the eternal wonders of his character and capabilities.

The coming consummation of the Kingdom of Jesus is a new world order where these ten longings are met decisively. How do I know this? It was all shown to John in the visions that are recorded in Revelation, the last book of the Bible.

Let me give you the highlights. (Theologians differ on the sequence of end-time events but they agree that the outcome is a perfect new world with a new human family united in love.)

When Jesus returns, there will be a major battle against evil, and the judgments of God will fill the earth. The faithful will rise to eternal life with Jesus, and those without a relationship of faith in Jesus will experience eternal judgment in the lake of fire. Then God will create the new heavens and the new earth. Check this out:

Then I saw a new heaven and a new earth, for the first heaven and the first earth had passed away, and there was no longer any sea. I saw the Holy City, the new Jerusalem, coming down out of heaven from God, prepared as a bride beautifully dressed for her husband. And I heard a loud voice from the throne saying, "Look! God's dwelling place is now among the people, and he will dwell with them. They will be his people, and God himself will be with them and be their God. He will wipe every tear from their eyes. There will be no more death or mourning or crying or pain, for the old order of things has passed away.[51]

Imagine no more pain, evil, tears, or death. Just eternal perfection.

---

[51] Revelation 21:1-5, NIV

I wasn't big on floating in the clouds with harps. But a pristine world to explore and a new resurrection body revved me up.

This body was described by Paul in one of his letters:

Our earthly bodies are planted in the ground when we die, but they will be raised to live forever. Our bodies are buried in brokenness, but they will be raised in glory. They are buried in weakness, but they will be raised in strength. They are buried as natural human bodies, but they will be raised as spiritual bodies.[52]

My new body will be perfect. I'll stand in the presence of God. I will never be sore or age. All my scars will be gone. Every filling and crooked tooth will be replaced by a perfect smile.

We can look at the resurrection appearances of Jesus to imagine what these new bodies might be like. He walked through walls and locked doors. He enjoyed eating. Some didn't recognize him until he spoke, so he must have gone from ordinary to amazing. Like him, we won't be married or have children in eternity.[53]

What will this new world be like? How old will we look? Will we all have perfect pitch voices? Will we all be able to run like Usain Bolt? Or faster? Will there be art and hiking and literature? What will it be like to swap stories with the men and women of history?

Or how about seeing the angels defeating the demons? Will there be a jumbotron replaying God's miracles and interventions? If you are curious for more about eternity, Randy Alcorn has written an amazing summary of all the Bible says about heaven, along with his biblically informed imagination.[54]

Here is the last part of John's amazing vision:

---

[52] 1 Corinthians 15:42-44, NLT
[53] See Luke 20:35
[54] See *Heaven* by Randy Alcorn.

Then the angel showed me the river of the water of life, as clear as crystal, flowing from the throne of God and of the Lamb down the middle of the great street of the city. On each side of the river stood the tree of life, bearing twelve crops of fruit, yielding its fruit every month. And the leaves of the tree are for the healing of the nations. No longer will there be any curse. The throne of God and of the Lamb will be in the city, and his servants will serve him. They will see his face, and his name will be on their foreheads. There will be no more night. They will not need the light of a lamp or the light of the sun, for the Lord God will give them light. And they will reign for ever and ever." [55]

Doesn't that awaken your soul and spirit?

A perfect city. No disease. A life of serving the King. No more night. All the renewable energy we need, simply given by the presence and glory of God. A new world. A new humanity living in harmony. A new universe, inviting creativity and discovery.

The Kingdom has echoed in our dreams, and all that has been expressed in art, literature, film, music, science, and exploration will come to pass. Our resurrection bodies will surpass anything that medicine, psychology, or AI could ever deliver. Bodies without deformities, injuries, or aging. No more pain, tears, evil, or sin. We will live in a stunning new world, complete with endless light and power, simply supplied by God's presence.

We are going to be thrilled beyond our wildest dreams.

Best of all, we will finally see God face to face. His presence will eclipse all the benefits of eternity. Being with God will be our single greatest reward - everything else will pale in comparison.

We will gaze on his life-giving beauty forever.

---

[55] Revelation 22:1-5, NIV

Moses was on the top of Mount Sinai with God twice for periods of 40 days and 40 nights. Each time, the Bible says he did not eat or drink![56] This is the sheer power of God's presence alone to perfectly sustain a rich and full life.

Those who trust Jesus will enjoy his Kingdom forever. We will become like him, knowing that humility is the way to greatness. The greatest in the Kingdom will be the ones who humbly serve and do not seek a name for themselves.[57] They will be honored by the Father.[58] This is just what Jesus modeled - he came not to be served but to serve.[59]

This early poem about Jesus describes his greatness:

The Son is the image of the invisible God, the firstborn over all creation. For in him all things were created: things in heaven and on earth, visible and invisible, whether thrones or powers or rulers or authorities; all things have been created through him and for him. He is before all things, and in him all things hold together.

And he is the head of the body, the church; he is the beginning and the firstborn from among the dead, so that in everything he might have the supremacy. For God was pleased to have all his fullness dwell in him, and through him to reconcile to himself all things, whether things on earth or things in heaven, by making peace through his blood, shed on the cross.[60]

Malcolm Muggeridge said it this way; "The good news of Jesus, then, was that the Kingdom of God had come and that he, Jesus, was its herald and expounder to men and women. More than that, in some special, mysterious way, he was the Kingdom."[61]

---

[56] See Deuteronomy 9:9 and 10:18
[57] Luke 22:24-26.
[58] John 12:26.
[59] Matthew 20:28.
[60] Colossians 1:15-20
[61] See *Jesus, The Man Who Lives*, 1976

What could possibly come close to Jesus and his Kingdom?

These discoveries transformed my life and my outlook. The future Jesus has earned for me is infusing every thought and every experience with hope and excitement.

When someone tells me "it doesn't get better than this" I know it's not true.

The best is yet to come and will exceed your wildest dreams.

Let his vision spark your life.

Jesus and His Kingdom is The Biggest Idea Ever.

Reflection question:

What emotions did you feel as you read this chapter?

Practical application:

If this chapter was a travel brochure, what preparations would you make for that trip?

Until Jesus returns, we can only see glimpses of the Kingdom. A great place to experience the Kingdom is in God's gift of community. Let's look at that next.

Chapter 8

Community: Lone Rangers Don't Flourish.

"If you want to go quickly, go alone.
If you want to go far, go together."

~ African proverb

"We are many parts of one body, and we all belong to each other."

~ The Apostle Paul

Community is a manifestation of the Kingdom, and crucial for a flourishing life.

One of the things that made the retreat such a great experience was the idea of grouping us at tables of six, with two facilitators who set clear ground rules for confidentiality. They asked good questions and listened well. They were skilled at drawing out our reactions, feelings, stories, and questions.

They were not uncomfortable with silence.

After each talk, we had time to journal. Then we were led with a well-crafted discussion prompt. Because the speakers had been so transparent, it fostered transparency at the table. The honesty reminded me of the Al-Anon meetings I attended to understand how best to live with my dad's drinking.

The weekend brought tears, laughter, prayers, confession, and encouragement. One guy who became a lifelong friend was Mike Ducker, who led FedEx in Asia. The guys called us the Kleenex Kids because of the constant flow of tears we shed all weekend. We had different life situations and issues to address, but we forged a bond of brotherhood that endures today.

The retreat taught me about the power of a small group to:

- help one another safely share feelings.

- gently confront our shortcomings.

- encourage and build each other up.

- get wisdom from the counsel of others.

- keep each other accountable.

I never had this kind of community.

On the last day, the leaders invited us to form follow-up groups. I ended up in a group with Mike and Elmer and four other guys. We met the very next Saturday morning at the American Club near Stanley Beach at 6 a.m. and did so weekly for the rest of my time in Hong Kong.

These meetings were powerful. We had two pastors and five business executives. In the first meeting, we did personal introductions, exchanged contact info, shared our key takeaways from the retreat and prayed for each other.

The second meeting turned into a time of confession. Some of the guys had been following Jesus a long time, some a few years, and I was the newbie. Each of us was convicted of sin at the retreat, and we were all hungry for accountability and growth.

The pastors, to my surprise, led the way in confession. I had never seen spiritual leaders being vulnerable. Their confession of financial worry, spiritual pride, jealousy of other pastors, and lack of prayer opened the way for the rest of us.

Jesus was at work. I progressed from more obvious sin patterns like a foul mouth, gluttony, and sexual addiction, into deeper matters related to my inner thoughts and attitudes.

As the weeks went on, the men shared marriage troubles, financial uncertainty, and emotional outbursts. We also shared missed opportunities in fatherhood, Bible study, prayer, and telling others about Jesus. We kept going back to the Bible, receiving grace, encouraging each other, and committing to pray for each other throughout the coming week.

It was transformative having these guys in my life. Because I knew I was going to see them every Saturday morning and give an unvarnished report on my week, I had the focus, desire, and accountability to start breaking my bad habits. We asked each other some key questions every week:

Am I seeking God in Scripture and prayer?

Am I loving my wife and kids well?

Am I giving my best at work?

Am I aware of people who may be hurting or in need?

Am I being generous with my time and money?

Am I refraining from catering to my appetites?

Am I careful about what I'm viewing?

Am I resting well?

Am I sharing the good news of Jesus?

Was I 100% honest with my answers?

At the end of one meeting, I ran into my boss Dimitri's wife Sue, and she asked me what our meeting was all about. I told her we were at a retreat recently and had decided to follow Jesus together and seek to be better husbands, dads, leaders at work, and members of our community.

It was the first time I had been asked to explain what had happened and what I was up to outside my family and small group. Sue was warm, curious, and asked good questions. Our discussion was very brief, but it felt great to share with someone I knew and appreciated.

I had opportunities to share what was going on at work. And I was tested too! I had several memorable interactions.

I told Dimitri what happened at the retreat and the impact it had on me. He was genuinely interested and shared his own spiritual heritage. We would have many more conversations about the Kingdom over the years.

Allen Clauss was my R&D leader. When I brought him up to speed, he smiled wryly. A PhD in chemical engineering, he had come to faith as a doctoral student. He was captivated by the growing evidence for the creation of the universe by an intelligent designer and had been following Jesus ever since.

Nathan Estruth was one of my key Brand Managers. His wife Madonna headed up our Market Research team. They had been following Jesus a long time and were excited for my new life. They were going through a significant trial with a newborn son with special needs, yet still reflected the joy and hope of the Kingdom. Their lives and prayers spoke volumes to me.

Steve Daines was our product supply logistics manager. He too was a follower of Jesus and was an encouraging example to me. All these colleagues were outstanding leaders in their fields of responsibility, and they helped me grow.

Jesus had cleaned up my foul mouth almost instantly, but it was always embarrassing when I got angry about a problem, talked negatively about another manager, or spouted cuss words when frustrated. These teammates saw me fail, and privately challenged and encouraged me.

Initially, I felt a bit like Bambi. I was awkward and could barely stand straight on my new faith's wobbly legs. This new life was unfamiliar territory. Changes were happening inside me. Ideas from the Scriptures had flipped the script of my life. The newness of it all made me unsteady, and there was no faking it.

On the road, I found my old habits beckoning me. Food, drink, and the ubiquitous porn offerings. By grace and prayer, pictures of my family displayed on my TV, coworkers praying for me, and knowing I'd meet the brothers Saturday morning, I learned to say no to my appetites and feed instead on the presence of Jesus and reading the Bible.

I was learning first-hand that the Kingdom of God is designed to be lived in community. My life as a Lone Ranger had come to an end. Paul described God's community vision to the church in Rome. What a masterpiece of wisdom:

Therefore, I urge you, brothers and sisters, in view of God's mercy, to offer your bodies as a living sacrifice, holy and pleasing to God—this is your true and proper worship. Do not conform to the pattern of this world, but be transformed by the renewing of your mind. Then you will be able to test and approve what God's will is—his good, pleasing and perfect will.

For by the grace given me I say to every one of you: Do not think of yourself more highly than you ought, but rather think of yourself with sober judgment, in accordance with the faith God has distributed to each of you. For just as each of us has one body with many members, and these members do not all have the same function, so in Christ we, though many, form one body, and each member belongs to all the others.[62]

---

[62] Romans 12:1-5, NIV

Jesus has given everything to rescue us, and in view of that mercy, Paul urged the believers in Rome to put their lives on the metaphorical altar of worship. In other words, live for God and others, and don't follow your old selfish patterns.

But exactly how are we to do this?

Paul says to renew your mind by replacing the thinking of the crowd with God's wisdom. The Bible displays his will—that's how to please him. Start with humility and recognize that because we were redeemed by Jesus, we belong to him and to each other.

No more going it alone.

Even God is not a Lone Ranger—he flows in perfect harmony as God the Father, the God-Man Jesus, and God the Holy Spirit. God is three-in-one—a perfect community of love, honor, purity, and seamless unity. He wants us to experience the very same bonds of community he enjoys.

It was a great relief to learn that I was not alone. God was healing my marriage and bringing me closer to my kids. He gave me a wonderful community of brothers. He also put people around me in the workplace, in my congregation, and my family. They were all ahead of me in the spiritual journey, but I was hungry and excited. They shared wisdom; I shared zeal.

Most of the Bible's advice is intended for groups. The "you" that we often see in Scripture is almost always plural. Let's continue with Paul's letter to the community in Rome:

Love must be sincere. Hate what is evil; cling to what is good.

Be devoted to one another in love. Honor one another above yourselves.

Never be lacking in zeal, but keep your spiritual fervor, serving the Lord.

Be joyful in hope, patient in affliction, faithful in prayer.

Share with the Lord's people who are in need. Practice hospitality.

Bless those who persecute you; bless and do not curse.

Rejoice with those who rejoice; mourn with those who mourn.

Live in harmony with one another.

Do not be proud but be willing to associate with people of low position. Do not be conceited.

Do not repay anyone evil for evil. Be careful to do what is right in the eyes of everyone.

If it is possible, as far as it depends on you, live at peace with everyone.

Do not take revenge, my dear friends, but leave room for God's wrath, for it is written:

"It is mine to avenge; I will repay," says the Lord.

On the contrary: "If your enemy is hungry, feed him; if he is thirsty, give him something to drink."

Do not be overcome by evil but overcome evil with good.[63]

This is the radical code for the Kingdom community of Jesus.

I wanted to reframe my life to become this kind of person. But there are a couple of dozen commands there. It wasn't practical to carry a list around. I needed a change of thinking, and the starting point was love. God calls us to engage with others and to love them. Jesus brought plenty of opportunities to practice.

Let me share two.

---

[63] Romans 12:9-21, NIV

I was wrestling with making a full confession to Marianne. But what were my motives? It would be selfish to just try and get things off my chest for my own sake, while crushing her. I did not want to hurt her more than I already had. I feared that she would want to divorce me, as she had said so early on in our marriage. Not a straightforward decision.

As I learned more, my hate for my infidelity grew. My disgust was fueled by many verses speaking to my sexual sin. This passage resonated particularly deeply with me:

Flee from sexual immorality. All other sins a person commits are outside the body, but whoever sins sexually, sins against their own body. Do you not know that your bodies are temples of the Holy Spirit, who is in you, whom you have received from God? You are not your own; you were bought at a price. Therefore honor God with your bodies.[64]

I had a vision of our marriage bed, soiled by my sin, and Jesus standing over it to blast it with light. He reminded me that he died for my sexual sin, and that in his grace, my marriage bed was now redeemed. This was the marriage I craved, and the marriage Marianne deserved.

I knew that the way to rebuild our marriage was to pray, zealously guard my purity, and serve Marianne in every way possible. That became my agenda, and over time she started seeing the kind of changes in me that I had noticed in her.

As to my wrestling about whether to confess everything to Marianne, the brothers gave me wise counsel that echoed what Elmer had told me the night I met Jesus. They told me, "Wait for the Spirit to lead you; you will know it when he settles that matter. Keep searching your motives and wait for clarity."

---

[64] 1 Corinthians 6:18-20, NIV

That was good counsel—stay out of God's way, let him lead.

A few months later, we met missionaries who had founded a children's shelter in the Philippines city of Cebu. Paul and Marlys were humble, determined leaders who cared for 70 children, many with special needs. Over the years, God had provided miraculously for these kids, often in the nick of time. We were invited to visit, and so the entire Beausejour family got ready to make our first mission trip.

As we read about the home ahead of time, we learned about a special eleven-year-old boy named Jake who had a severe case of cerebral palsy. He was in his bed for much of the day, with muscles so taut that he had great difficulty sitting up or eating.

For some reason we thought a red sportscar bed we had would be a blessing for him and make him feel special. Paul and Marlys agreed it was a great idea. So off we went to Cebu with clothes, shoes, bulging suitcases, stuffed back packs, and a crazy looking kid's bed wrapped with cardboard and tape.

The trip transformed our entire family.

We got to meet Jake, read to him, hug him, hang out in his room, and bring him to the dining area to have a meal with him. He was so intelligent with responsive sparkling eyes, and he understood much of what was going on. But he was trapped in an unresponsive body that was taut like a high wire.

Jake loved eating! His food flew all over the place as he waved his spoon wildly. He just smiled. My kids loved it. On the second day we put together the race car bed and swapped it in place of his old bed. You should have seen his joy and excitement; he was shaking and wiggling all over the place. And the other kids celebrated and cheered. It was a holy moment.

The kids' schedule included school, Bible study, sports time, and chores. There were music lessons, art lessons, and times of sharing after dinner. One night, Arlene, a blind 16-year-old girl, stood up after dinner and recited the first three chapters of Genesis. Another evening, the children stood up and sang a beautiful thank you song.

Near the end of our visit, I took Jake for a walk in a special stroller. I could communicate with him clearly on an emotional level, feeling his love, respect, care, and faith. I carried Jake in my heart for years until his death. He lived much longer than expected no doubt because of the love he gave and received. In the world he was unknown and of low position, but in the economy of the Kingdom he was a rich and famous man.

We were changed forever in Cebu.

Our kids fell in love with their new friends, got wrapped up in the flow of the kids' lives there, and did not want to leave. As we got into the minibus for the ride to the airport, my heart was bursting.

Each of my kids jumped in, waving wildly. They had shorts and t-shirts but nothing else. They had given away their shoes, backpacks, baseball caps, clothes, and their hearts.

We need community! I am so glad I am no longer a Lone Ranger. I'm learning to leave the lie of self-sufficiency.

Reflection question:

How do you feel about the quality of community in your life?

Practical application:

Who could help you build a flourishing community?

Community brings us together, but human nature means that we will have problems in our journey of growth and healing. Every person and every community will need two crucial gifts to stay healthy, safe, and free. Let's look at those next.

.

Chapter 9
Living Freely: Two Crucial Gifts.

"Repentance is ultimate honesty."

~ Dietrich Bonhoeffer

"Forgiveness flounders because I exclude my enemy from the community of humans and myself from the community of sinners."

~ Miroslav Volf

Repentance and forgiveness are two key gifts Jesus has given to help us stay on the path to freedom. Without these gifts, my life, marriage, and family would have been destroyed. What God did was nothing short of miraculous.

I was settling into the rhythms of community and getting used to new ways of daily life. In late May, Dimitri called me into his office to tell me about my next assignment at P&G.

To my surprise, we were being transferred to Cincinnati, where I would take the role of VP Advertising. I would be responsible for the company's brand advertising work, relationships with advertising agencies, and providing staff leadership for the marketing community.

It was a fantastic assignment with a very high profile.

I would no longer be responsible for an operating division's profit and loss. This was my first staff role, which would require leadership by example, expertise, and service.

I was stepping into the big shoes of well-respected predecessors. Bob Goldstein had been influential in my growth as a Brand Manager and advertising practitioner. It was a huge loss when

Bob died in a rafting accident in 1987. Ross Love succeeded Bob and did an amazing job. He was leaving P&G to build a radio station network, which became the largest owned by an African American in the US.

Things were moving fast. We made a school and house-hunting trip in late May 1996 and packed up our belongings in early June. Marianne and the kids spent June and July in Canada while I handed off my business in China. I took the first week of August for family vacation, then started my new job while Marianne unpacked the house and got kids ready for their new school.

It was an exciting time for our family. A lot happened in Hong Kong before we left. It was a season of significant repentance. Jesus was doing a thorough spring cleaning in my heart. My confession with Elmer was just the beginning.

My conscience had become very sensitive.

Jesus started his ministry by saying, *"The time has come, the kingdom of God has come near. Repent and believe the good news!"*[65]

Jesus was opening the Kingdom to all those who would repent and believe his good news.

What does it mean to repent? The word has a connotation of penance and punishment. Movies like *The Mission* portray repentance as an act of self-flagellation. But that is a product of translation influenced by the Latin word *paenitere*.

The word in Greek is *metanoia*. It means to think differently, to reconsider, to change one's mind, and to turn decisively away from previous thoughts and behaviors. It involves the mind and the will and translates into actions.

---

[65] Mark 1:15, NIV

Metanoia was used brilliantly in the Apple "Think Different" campaign that invited us, along with Einstein and Gandhi, to rethink computers. Metanoia comes with changes in perception, understanding, belief, and commitment.

We receive the Kingdom when we see Jesus for who he really is and place our faith in him. We are born again; we experience a transformation and a regeneration of our inner being. As we experience him, we begin to see the world differently. The Scriptures touch us and renew our mind, which changes the way we process reality.

Repentance is a gift from a kind God.[66]

Repentance began happening in my heart as I processed my near-death experience in Japan. I knew something deep was broken in my life, but I was not able to change until I had a coherent model to replace it with.

Jesus explained the world's brokenness. His teaching, sacrificial death, and resurrection provided a powerful, inspirational, and rational solution to my selfishness and alienation.

As I began to admit my brokenness, confess my wrongdoing, and make changes in my beliefs and behaviors, my thinking, priorities, and relationships improved. I had a sense of wonder as I saw the world in a new way.

I had such a lightness of life.

This is *eudaemonia*, the Good Life and happiness the Greek philosophers sought. It is the deep joy that the Bible promises when we are right with God. Jesus takes great joy in our repentance and gladly grants forgiveness and cleansing.

---

[66] Romans 2:4 NIV

However, things were more complicated with Marianne. She knew my life was changing in significant ways, and our relationship was growing in so many dimensions. I did not want to hurt her.

One morning I read the story in Genesis about the first marriage:

But for Adam no suitable helper was found. So the Lord God caused the man to fall into a deep sleep; and while he was sleeping, he took one of the man's ribs and then closed up the place with flesh. Then the Lord God made a woman from the rib he had taken out of the man, and he brought her to the man. The man said, "This is now bone of my bones and flesh of my flesh; she shall be called 'woman,' for she was taken out of man."

That is why a man leaves his father and mother and is united to his wife, and they become one flesh. Adam and his wife were both naked, and they felt no shame.[67]

The last verse popped off the page into my heart. I was deeply repentant for my infidelity. I was totally confident that Jesus had purified our marriage bed. I was just constantly aware that something was between us. I was waiting on God, and the moment of his choosing came very suddenly.

It was unmistakably a supernatural and holy moment.

Our Hong Kong townhouse had a small private pool. With Hong Kong's constant heat and humidity, we often took an evening swim before turning in. Usually this was a quick skinny dip. As we walked into the water, I was overcome by the Spirit and began sobbing. Marianne asked, "What's the matter Denis?"

I stammered through my confession of infidelity, without going into every detail, but hitting all the highlights of when, where, how often, and to my best ability, the roots of this deficiency in my character. I kept it brief, fully realizing that I was dumping a

---

[67] Genesis 2:20-25, NIV

big ugly load on her. I explained why I had waited so long, my conflicted emotions about hurting her, and all the negative consequences this had meant for her, our marriage, and our family. I pledged to never do it again and told her I had men holding me accountable to end the bad habits that led to my sin.

I shared how the verse from Genesis had pricked my conscience, and how Jesus had given me clarity and hope for the purity of our relationship. Then I said, "Will you forgive me?" There was a long moment of silence.

Her pain was palpable. She looked up and prompted by the Lord, said, "The Lord has forgiven everything I have done. So, I forgive you". Light prevailed, and my shame began to lift.

It wasn't easy. Marianne was processing the hurt. She asked a lot of questions. I gave her all the details she asked for. I owned all the negative consequences that had accrued to her and asked for her forgiveness any time a new detail became known. I asked if there was anything else she wanted me to do to better reflect my desire to make things right. Slowly, we worked through the damage.

Then one sunny morning, she woke up and let me know she had worked through it, and we were done. She would not hold anything against me or ever remind me of my sin. She forgave me as far as the east is from the west (she was quoting Psalm 103:12). Not only did Jesus lead her response; he showed her that he was working in my life.

Marianne has often reminded me of little things I have done that irked her. Like the time I cleaned a pile of old mail off her desk, and inadvertently threw out a $100 bill she had in there. Whenever my "neat freak" invades her "pack rat" spaces, she gets very touchy. I've heard about that $100 bill quite a few times!

But since that day, she has never brought up my adultery. Yes, we have told many people our story, but I share about my sin, and she shares her forgiveness. This gift of the Kingdom has shaped the trajectory of our family. In her giving me grace, we started over and gave our marriage and our future to Jesus. We made the King and his Kingdom the center of our family.

Three decades later, we have a strong family anchored in Jesus and his Kingdom. Our four kids know our story, and we always honor the fact that our family stands on the good news of Jesus and Marianne's obedience in forgiving me.

We do our best to practice repentance and forgiveness as a family. We are teaching our grandchildren the Kingdom Good News and the same joys of repentance and forgiveness.

God cleared the way just before we moved to Cincinnati.

His timing was perfect.

I met Ken Blanchard soon after we moved, at one of his "Lead Like Jesus" seminars. Ken was famous for his little book *The One Minute Manager* published in 1982. It was a favorite at P&G. In the 1990s Ken discovered the Kingdom, and as he describes it, "I suited up for Jesus".

As his understanding of the Bible grew, he realized that he had not dealt with the possibility that the One Minute Manager might be wrong occasionally. So, in 2002, he published the *One Minute Apology*, a wonderful resource for encouraging repentance in the workplace.[68]

Later, I attended a seminar led by my old friend Ford Taylor. His take on biblical repentance was powerful.[69] Inspired by Ford's

---

[68] See leadlikejesus.com
[69] See Ford Taylor, *Relational Leadership: When relationships collide with transactions.*

110

work, we adopted a social covenant to guide our interactions in repentance and forgiveness, taking Jesus' path to freedom from the sins we all regularly commit. This social covenant has done so much good to help us maintain a healthy and vibrant community and has done wonders with marriage and parenting challenges. Marianne and I say it often: God's way works!

Kingdom repentance requires deep humility and truth. These six detailed steps will help you practice repentance well:

1. Acknowledge what we did by stating the offense without excuses. ("I did 'it'")

2. Admit that we are wrong, even if the other person is also wrong. ("I was wrong")

3. Say that we are sorry for our actions and their effect. ("I am sorry for how this affected you, with specific examples")

4. Ask for forgiveness: "Will you forgive me?" or "If and when you can, will you forgive me?"

5. Ask the person: "Will you hold me accountable? I give you permission to do so."

6. Make things right, then ask: "Is there anything else I can do to better reflect my repentance?"

Kingdom forgiveness requires deep humility and grace. These six practical steps will help you forgive well:

1. We won't carry a superior, self-justifying attitude, and we won't caricature the other person.

2. We truly believe that we are also capable of these things!

3. We take pity—put our heart out to the other—and identify with them in their weakness.

4. We will cancel the debt, absorb the cost, turn it over to Jesus, and let our feelings catch up.

5. We will let them go in freedom—we will not hold a grudge or keep a record of wrongs.

6. We will actively seek the other person's blessing in prayer, word, and deed.

Two things have always stood out to me about these two gifts.

First, it is impossible to enter the Kingdom without genuine repentance. Jesus invites everyone, but only receives those who acknowledge their sin and see their need for a redeemer. In our sin, we feel distant from God, but counter-intuitively, the only remedy is to run to him with it.

Second, when we forgive sin, we aren't approving of it. We simply absorb the debt, give up on vengeance, and turn it over to Jesus. Forgiveness sets us free from the bitterness that will set in if we hang on to the offense.

Repentance and forgiveness are hard and humbling, but they are crucial to living freely. Here's an example of what I mean.

Soon after moving to Cincinnati, I was in contact with an old friend who worked at McDonald's with me. After our chat, I started reflecting on my college days working at McDonald's. It was a challenging time. I worked 4-5 days a week, usually for 8-10 hours. I ate at McDonald's dozens of times every week. I was frequently out of cash and dropped in often to get a free meal when I was not working.

Jesus showed me this was stealing.

There were hundreds of meals over a four-year period. And drinks. Occasionally I brought friends. On late-night shifts when I did the deposits, I took out the American dollars that we would get because

US tour buses stopped for food. We did not give any exchange, but the banks and some retailers like gas stations gave 10-15%. So, I replaced the American dollars with Canadian currency and profited from my thieving arbitrage.

I tallied the total theft, and it was a few thousand dollars. But that was 20 years beforehand. The Lord said, "OK business major, what about the interest?" Ka-Ching, and the total came to $9,750. My heart was pounding. Every bone in my body wanted to justify my theft with all kinds of excuses.

The hardest thing was to own it. Recognize my wrong and admit it. Putting my pride aside, I knew my next step was to tell Marianne and make things right with my old boss Rick Hession. It was humbling and embarrassing. I had lost track of Rick but found an address for his new restaurant in Colorado.

I wrote Rick about my newfound faith and my utter loathing of what I had done behind his back. I felt deep regret for my actions and asked him to forgive me. I told him I would never do this again. I knew Rick did not need the money, but I just prayed that my action would convey repentance and a full desire to make things right with the man who had done so much for me.

Rick called me shortly afterward. He was indeed shocked by my confession. He forgave me and said that my actions were sufficient. He gave the money to the ministry of Paul Henderson.

Paul was a famous Canadian professional hockey player who scored the winning goals in the last three games of the 1972 Cold War Summit Series between Canada and the Soviet Union. Paul had found meaning and focus after hockey through a decision to follow Jesus. He became nationally known by his passion for telling people about Jesus and his Kingdom.

Jesus took my sin and repentance and turned it into something good. When I talk to Rick on the phone now, our relationship is restored, and we have warm conversation and prayer.

You might be thinking, "What happens if the person you are dealing with is not responsive?"

Practically, it is not always possible to complete the repentance and forgiveness process. In the case of my theft, Rick could have chosen to ignore my letter. Sometimes there is so much pain that people break off relationships. Sometimes there is pride and arrogance. Sometimes death interrupts the process.

In cases where you've made every reasonable effort, you can rest in peace even if the person does not respond. Remember the wonderful counsel we looked at earlier:

If it is possible, as far as it depends on you, live at peace with everyone. Do not take revenge, my dear friends, but leave room for God's wrath, for it is written: "It is mine to avenge; I will repay," says the Lord.[70]

What good counsel to forget about revenge. So much energy and effort are wasted on revenge. Remember *Les Misérables*? Jean Valjean found freedom in forgiveness, but his vengeful antagonist Javert only found misery.

Forgiveness is for your own good, to release the debt to Jesus and to avoid the bitterness that comes with unforgiveness. It is also a prerequisite for your own sins to be forgiven:

For if you forgive other people when they sin against you, your heavenly Father will also forgive you. But if you do not forgive others their sins, your Father will not forgive your sins.[71]

Unforgiveness puts you into spiritual checkmate. In the unique economy of the Kingdom, forgiveness brings as much freedom

---

[70] Romans 12:18-19, NIV
[71] Matthew 6:14-15, NIV

as repentance. We need both these gifts to experience all that Jesus did for us.

If you want to live freely, be a repentant forgiver.

I'll close this chapter with a story to show you the limitless power of the Gospel of King Jesus.

Let me take you back to the end of World War II, and the famous Nuremberg Trials of the Nazi leaders for their crimes against humanity. Hitler, Himmler, and Goebbels had already committed suicide. Twenty-one top leaders were on trial in the first round; 15 were Protestant while 6 were Roman Catholic.

A Lutheran pastor from Missouri named Henry Gerecke had been serving in a military hospital in Germany. He was assigned as Chaplain to the 15 Protestant prisoners.

He was chosen because he was Lutheran, experienced in prison ministry, and he spoke German fluently. He had three sons in the US military, two of whom were injured by the Germans. He saw these men as lost souls and felt God wanted him to minister to them. What a Jesus-like attitude.

Gerecke met with the 15 men individually in their cells between November 12, 1945, and October 1, 1946, when the verdicts of the court were given. He ministered to those who requested his support. Hess and Rosenberg declined and never engaged.

The other 13 attended Sunday services, but for many, it was just an excuse to get out of their cells. Prisoners Goering, Doenitz, Von Neurath, Schacht, and Funk did not receive the Gospel. But gradually, over the next 10 months, prisoners Keitel, Sauckel, Raeder, Ribbentrop, Fritsche, Schirach, Frick, and Speer repented and received the Good News of Jesus.

Pastor Gerecke was very careful to wait until true signs of repentance had occurred. He was an experienced prison minister and knew what a phony show of sorrow looked like.

The court's verdicts included death by hanging for six, life in prison for three, extended prison terms for four, while two were found not guilty.

Based on Gerecke's experienced testimony, we can confidently say that eight of these criminals were declared "not guilty" in the court of the Kingdom. They repented and received Jesus' payment for their sin. By faith, they received eternal life. The other seven refused the Good News of Jesus and will pay their own penalty in eternity.[72]

There will be many surprises in heaven.

Prostitutes, murderers, adulterers, and liars will be there, saved by their faith in a great King. Some Nazi war criminals will be there, saved by the same faith in the great King. There will be boastful and brutal kings like Babylon's Nebuchadnezzar, who finally bent the knee to the greatest King.

Jesus and his Kingdom is the biggest idea ever to cross the horizon of history. Jesus forgives the truly repentant, even the worst of sinners.

There will be no one in heaven who thought they were a good person, worthy on their own merits. There will be no one who trusted that their good deeds outweighed their bad deeds.

Only repentant people who have trusted in Jesus and received his forgiving grace will be in heaven. All others will be eternally separated from God.

---

[72] See http://www.messianicgoodnews.org/henry-gerecke-chaplain-to-nazi-war-criminals/

Reflection question:

Is anything holding you back from repenting of your sins and seeking forgiveness, or from forgiving those who have hurt you?

Practical application:

Repent of all your sins. Ask Jesus to forgive you. Make amends with those you can. You will notice a lightness you never had.

Forgive everyone who has sinned against you. In time, you will experience the freedom and lightness only Jesus can give you.

To help with our repentance and forgiveness, and to activate our life together, Jesus has given us a powerful helper. He is called the Counselor or the Advocate, and some even call him the Wild Goose. Let's meet him now.

Chapter 10

Wild Goose: The Antidote to Burnout.

"The early Celtic Christians called the Holy Spirit 'the wild goose.' And the reason why is that they knew that you cannot tame him."

~ John Eldredge

"You will receive power when the Holy Spirit comes on you."

~ Jesus of Nazareth

Our family was settling into life in Cincinnati. Marianne and the kids were thriving. I loved my new job. The "Wild Goose" was empowering me to put the ways of Jesus into practice.

The process of reorienting my priorities and walking in my new habits was going well. The Spirit was bringing the Bible to life. This poetic verse inspired me and became my life's anthem:

He has made everything beautiful in its time.

He has also set eternity in the human heart;

yet no one can fathom what God has done from beginning to end.[73]

That verse captures the awe of God's genius as revealed in the universe. It captures our ability as humans to grasp the idea of eternity. We can see it in the sunrise or sunset on a sprawling beach, the majesty of towering mountain peaks, the impact of music and art, the climax of a man and his wife making love, the sound of waves lapping, or a night sky filled with stars. We sense the beauty of God's handiwork and are filled with awe. Yet we can't fully grasp the vastness and mystery of God's works.

---

[73] Ecclesiastes 3:11, NIV

By placing eternity in our hearts, the Creator gave us the ability to imagine his power, knowledge, and presence everywhere. Yet this ability creates a vacuum of yearning desires from within. By design, only God can fill that eternal vacuum. Until we know this, we try to fill that eternal donut hole in vain.

The author of that passage was the brilliant and uber-wealthy King Solomon, who ruled the sprawling Israeli empire in the tenth century BC. Solomon had unlimited resources to experiment on filling the eternal hole in his heart.

He tried the best food and wine, music, dancers, and entertainers. He had the world's most powerful military. He built great projects—a palace, a temple, homes, gardens, parks, and cities. He owned vast flocks and herds.

He collected gold and silver worth billions today. He studied zoology and botany, and his fleet of ships brought wildlife and plants from all over the known world. He wrote many songs and proverbs. Solomon's content anchors the Bible's repository of ancient Jewish wisdom - the book of Proverbs.

Yet he married 700 women and had 300 concubines. Do you see the irony? It's hard to imagine a wise man taking on 700 mothers-in-law! Solomon did not finish well because he got distracted by all these women and their pagan gods.

Solomon's book of Ecclesiastes is a masterpiece of existential philosophy. Solomon is an Epicurean at the start but finishes like a Stoic. He concludes that his life is fleeting, like vapor or mist.

Unable to fill the hole in his heart, Solomon was distracted and grew distant from God. In the end, he saw that his life was wasted and that the key to life is to know, love, and obey God. He had burned out on exhaustion, futility, and dread.

I spent my life stuffing food, drink, sex, achievement, knowledge, money, possessions, and success into that eternal hole in my heart. Like Solomon, it left me empty and unsatisfied. The discovery of Jesus and his Kingdom finally filled that eternal hole.

Exactly how does this hole in our hearts get filled?

The answer to this question revolves around the work of the Holy Spirit. We meet the Spirit in the second verse of the Bible:

Now the earth was formless and empty, darkness was over the surface of the deep, and the Spirit of God was hovering over the waters.[74]

The Holy Spirit is the third person who is addressed as God in the Bible, along with the Father and the Son. God has revealed that he exists in three persons but is One. You may have heard this expressed in the word "Trinity". That word is not in the Bible, but the Bible affirms repeatedly that God is One. It also affirms that he is three distinct people.

How this all works, only God knows.

Each of these three amazing beings are uncreated, without origin. They have never learned anything or had anything occur to them. They self-exist without needing anything. They are always on the same page.

The Father, Son and Holy Spirit have always been a united community. They cooperated in creation seamlessly. They are cooperating in sustaining the creation and in the advancement of the Kingdom of God through history. All three are equally God, but each voluntarily takes different roles.

The Father takes the role of family head, and he sends the Son to become a human being to rescue us. The Father pronounced

---

[74] Genesis 1:2, NIV

his deep love and satisfaction with Jesus when he was baptized. In that moment we see the Trinity in action. The Father spoke his love, and the Spirit rested on Jesus in the form of a dove.

The Father poured out his wrath on Jesus instead of us. Imagine how hard it would be to sentence your son to death. The Father declares anyone who believes in Jesus is not guilty of sin because Jesus paid their debt. Believers are adopted into the Father's eternal family, with their name written in the book of life. The Father is collecting a family through the work of Jesus. There is nothing like coming home to the Father.

Jesus is the Word that spoke the creation into being. Jesus rules both the first creation and the new creation that began when he rose from the grave in his resurrection body.

One day, every enemy of God will be under the feet of Jesus. The celebration at the end of this age will be in honor of Jesus as his followers are united with him at his wedding banquet. The Bible describes human marriage as a metaphor for the coming together of Jesus (the groom) with his followers (the bride).

In the end, Jesus will hand the Kingdom back to his Father. In the meantime, Jesus assigns us the mission of going out and sharing the Good News with our "not yet" brothers and sisters. They are added to the Father's family by faith.

The Holy Spirit has more of a supporting role behind the scenes. Because of that, he has been called the forgotten God.[75] The Holy Spirit appears periodically in the Old Testament. He fills a few selected people, mostly prophets, priests, and kings, who perform miracles and write the Scriptures. The prophets speak of the age when the Holy Spirit will play a more major role. This was fulfilled

---

[75] See *The Forgotten God* by Francis Chan, an excellent explanation of the work of the Spirit.

ten days after Jesus ascended to the Father in heaven. The Holy Spirit fell on Jesus' followers, empowering them to bring the Good News of Jesus and his Kingdom to the world.

Through the pages of the New Testament, the Holy Spirit appears about 400 times. Even now, he fills every believer so we can fulfill the mission of the Father and Son. The Bible tells us the amazing things the Spirit does. The Scriptures helped me to understand my own experiences and what to ask for in prayer.

Remember the words of Jesus about being born again? This is one of the core activities of the Holy Spirit. As he hovered over the waters during creation, he now hovers over us, wooing us towards Jesus. The Spirit gives our human spirit the new life of the Kingdom. We experience the love, joy, and peace of God by the work of the Holy Spirit. That's why I felt like my insides were exploding. I was being re-born by the Holy Spirit!

Without the Spirit's rebirth no one can see the Kingdom.

As I began to believe the Kingdom's Good News, God the Spirit had begun moving into my life. Only his infinite life could begin to fill that eternal hole in my heart. I could not walk into the Kingdom until the Spirit moved on me and began to fill me up. The Spirit wooed me toward Jesus - he's like a tractor beam.

The Spirit was changing me from the inside out.

The Spirit sealed my adoption by the Father into the family of God. I was living life like an orphan, working overtime for my own security under a foolish vow of self-sufficiency. The opening of the Kingdom brought me into a fabulous family with a Father who loves me. I was drawn into his community by the Spirit! The best version of me was redefined: 1) adopted by the Father; 2) abiding in the Son's presence; and 3) anointed by the Holy Spirit.

Renovated and remade by the Trinity!

I experience the Spirit's presence whenever I meet with other followers of Jesus. It was no accident that I became life-long friends with my Hong Kong brothers. So, it was a priority to find a community in Cincinnati. Marianne found out about a church that sounded like a great fit for our family.

On our first Sunday, I asked for some guys to connect with, and I began meeting with Kerry Bradley and Kerry Olin within the first month I was in the city. We met almost every Saturday morning for the next eight years. I am so thankful for these guys investing in my growth, and their life-long friendship.

The Spirit continued his work as he enabled me to leave my sinful ways behind. This is why my filthy language changed so quickly and effortlessly. This is why I could kick the porn habit and why I never went back to it. This is why I am no longer a glutton. I love food, but I am down fifty pounds to the weight I was on my wedding day. The Spirit helps me understand the Kingdom and gives me the power to obey Jesus.

The Spirit fuels the cycle of repentance and forgiveness. When we sin, we quench the Spirit. He is still with us, but we feel a loss of joy, power, and fullness. There is no more condemnation for our sin, but we can feel a loss of relational quality. The Spirit leads us into repentance and restores us. The Spirit gives us the grace to forgive, even when our emotions may lag. When we confess, forgive, and restore relationships, the Spirit cleanses our sin and refills our lives. That is what happened in our marriage.

The Spirit enables us to live the Kingdom lifestyle. Without the Spirit, following Jesus turns into a self-propelled checklist of rules and duties. Those who attempt to follow Jesus without the Spirit suffer burnout and frustration. Only the Spirit can help us love the unlovable. Only the Spirit can help us serve Jesus wholeheartedly. Only the Spirit pours the Father's love into our hearts and grants the patience Kingdom life requires.

Without the Spirit, I was experiencing burnout in China. Research suggests that 79% of people experience some level of burnout in their work. That burnout traces to exhaustion, feelings of futility, and absenteeism driven by avoidance.[76]

Spirit-walking is the Kingdom's antidote to burnout. The Spirit helped me keep my work in perspective, lifted my attitude, inspired new ideas, and gave me capacity to tackle conflict and problems, and the energy to encourage my co-workers.

The Spirit does this by gradually working his character qualities into our body, soul, and spirit. A few lists in the Bible describe these character traits. One list includes love, joy, peace, patience, kindness, goodness, gentleness, faithfulness, and self-control.[77] Another list includes faith, goodness, knowledge, self-control, perseverance, godliness, mutual affection, and love.[78]

You get the idea. These qualities are described as fruit of the Spirit. They overcome evil and keep us from stumbling. They make us more like Jesus. And like the Spirit, they help us point others to Jesus. When we are filled with the Spirit, people smell the fragrance of Jesus.[79] I call this lifestyle Spirit-Walking.

Cool things happen when we meet old friends we haven't seen in a while. They notice something different about you but can't describe it, like the way I experienced Marianne changing. It might take a few encounters, but they will often ask, "what happened to you?"

---

[76] https://www.octanner.com/global-culture-report/2020-burnout
[77] Galatians 5:22-23, NIV
[78] 2 Peter 1:5-7, NIV
[79] See 2 Corinthians 2:15, NLT

I ran into my old friend Fred in an airport. I hadn't seen him in years. After chatting a bit, he noticed that I had changed. I asked him what he meant. He said I was less cocky and arrogant, and my speaking volume was down about 60%. (I was more of a jerk than I remembered!)

Undeterred, I shared my story.

Losses had impacted his work, income, and satisfaction in life. I shared the Good News of the Kingdom with him and prayed for him. The Spirit was at work. Mark was in tears, yet we were both completely at ease despite being in a public place.

The Spirit distributes gifts—at least one—to every follower of Jesus. That day in a busy airport, the P&G exec brought healing and encouragement. Spiritual gifts are supernatural abilities that bring God's love to tangible expression in the lives of others.

I was in my office at P&G late one afternoon when one of our most talented leaders walked in and asked for a few minutes. I closed the door and listened carefully. She just found out her dad had a terminal diagnosis with weeks to live.

She was looking for counsel.

The Spirit showed me she regretted that they were not closer. I pulled an extra Bible out of my credenza and shared a few passages. I encouraged her to confess any regrets to him and ask for forgiveness. I helped her to forgive her dad, and to make a list of things to thank him for. With the Spirit's help, she left feeling encouraged and eager to get right with her father.

The Spirit is always associated with God's power. Jesus promised his followers that they would receive power when the Holy Spirit came on them, so they could accomplish his mission to reach the whole world.

As I continued learning, I came across this verse:

The Kingdom of God is not a matter of talk but of power.[80]

God was doing amazing things in my life. I was experiencing radical character change, the healing of my orphan mentality, enjoying rich community, and a restored marriage and family. But that verse went into my heart like an arrow. God was pointing out that there was even more power available in his Kingdom. I wanted what Jesus promised his disciples:

Very truly I tell you, whoever believes in me will do the works I have been doing, and they will do even greater things than these, because I am going to the Father. And I will do whatever you ask in my name, so that the Father may be glorified in the Son. You may ask me for anything in my name, and I will do it.[81]

So, I asked!

That prayer has been answered often over the years. I'm going to share a few of these miraculous stories. This is not to boast, but to show you the truth of Scripture and the grace of Jesus. Multitudes have experienced this power; I am not unique.

I was receiving prayer one night and the Holy Spirit came on me with power. I was knocked to the floor the way Paul was knocked off his horse on the road to Damascus. I was wide awake and aware of what was happening, but unable to move.

I felt a hand go in behind my neck and pull what felt like a part of my spinal cord out of my body. I blurted "That hurt! What is that?"

The person praying for me said, "Denis, that's the Spirit removing your selfish ambition. You won't be needing that anymore." I knew immediately that this character defect was still part of my makeup.

---

[80] 1 Corinthians 4:20, NIV
[81] John 14:12-14, NIV

No room for that in the Kingdom.

The Spirit gave insights for my work at P&G. I began to focus on the top global brands that delivered most of our sales and profit. I focused on two measures: our category value or dollar share and achieving declining marketing expenses as a percentage of sales.

These measures would drive us to offer superior performance and value, achieved with marketing strategies that were effective enough to produce margin growth. To reinforce this focus, we began rewarding our advertising agencies for sales growth.

The Spirit was speaking daily about my work.

God challenged me with assignments that required his power for healing - in church settings, and at work. We prayed for a young girl with anemia one Sunday at church, and on the next Tuesday, she called to say her Monday blood test showed normal results, and she had her energy back!

A woman at church complained about arthritis in her hands. I saw the word "unforgiveness" on her forehead. I asked her if there was anyone she needed to forgive. She burst into tears and said immediately "My brother. How did you know?" I explained the Spirit's nudge, and the links between unforgiveness and bitterness. I asked her if she would forgive her brother and trust that her feelings would follow. She forgave him and released the debt to Jesus. We prayed for the healing of her arthritis. She called the next day to tell me her pain was gone.

During a mission trip to Mexico, three siblings were brought to the children's home where we were serving. They had been in a violent home and had suffered trauma. The girls, aged 6-11, were tormented by evil spirits and were manifesting symptoms of shaking and fits of anger. We prayed that the calm of the Holy

Spirit would come over them in the name of Jesus. Then we asked them if they would give themselves to Jesus and learn to follow him in the community of their new home. They were relieved to have a loving place to live in and eagerly said yes. We then cast out the spirits in the name of Jesus.

The girls were set free.

Later, on a trip to Nigeria, we showed the *Jesus* film in a remote village. Afterward, people were invited to receive Jesus and his Kingdom. Dozens of people came forward, including many women carrying babies. The children had a respiratory virus and were gasping for air. We laid hands on their heaving chests, and instantly they were all healed.

When the townspeople saw this, they had us pray for stomach pain, kidney stones, headaches, sore knees, feet, and backs. They were relieved of pain and shouted and danced in gratitude.

As we were wrapping up, a mother brought her 10-year-old boy who was deaf from birth. I stuck my fingers in his ears and commanded them to open by the power of Jesus. He immediately jerked his head as the first sounds flowed through his ears to his brain. He was stunned, as I was, and ran around the village with glee.

My sister Patty struggled with substance abuse for years. After a long series of losses and disappointments, she attempted suicide. We were hundreds of miles apart, and our relationship was already strained so badly that she did not want a visit.

All we could do is pray. But God! A social worker who had recently emigrated from India was assigned by the provincial health care system to help Patty. Arun was a Spirit-filled believer—what a miracle, the proverbial needle in a haystack!

Arun patiently served Patty, finding government resources to benefit her. After hours, he visited and led her to Jesus and showed her the Spirit-filled life. Patty learned to Spirit-Walk and overcame her addictions by God's power.

Arun connected Patty to a small church that met weekly in a muffler shop. That group loved Patty and taught her more of the Spirit-Walking life! Patty joined AA and became a sought-after speaker in her area. She reached five years of sobriety and led many into the Kingdom before she passed from cancer.

The Holy Spirit's power is available to ordinary people who trust and follow Jesus. By learning how to Spirit-Walk, we can live the life Jesus promises, and escape the pit of burnout.

These stories may raise the question—why doesn't God heal all the time? I simply want to say that the Kingdom is here, but not fully until Jesus returns. We pray in faith—and sometimes God does not heal as we hope. Patty died of cancer, despite a lot of prayer and previous healing in her life. With an eternal perspective, we saw that in death she was healed for good.

These stories remind me that our brains can only take us so far with God. Only the Spirit can reveal the things of God:

The person without the Spirit does not accept the things that come from the Spirit of God but considers them foolishness and cannot understand them because they are discerned only through the Spirit.[82]

Followers of Jesus have unlimited access to the "Wild Goose". He is God. Untamable. He is the antidote to burnout because he provides peace, power, and contentment.

---

[82] See 1 Corinthians 2:14, NIV

Reflection question:

What would you most want the Holy Spirit to do in your life?

Practical application:

Ask Jesus to fill you with the Holy Spirit and watch God work!

The Kingdom was coming with power.

I soon realized Jesus wanted more of me.

Chapter 11
All In: Buy That Field!

*"Your greatest moments in life will be
the moments when you went all in."*

~ Mark Batterson

*"Those of you who do not give up everything you have
cannot be my disciples."*

~ Jesus of Nazareth

My passion for the Kingdom was a lot like the moment I knew I wanted to marry Marianne and spend the rest of my life with her. The Kingdom was the biggest idea ever, and it was moving from my head to captivate my heart.

Jesus was showing me how to live life to the full. He was the smartest, wisest, bravest leader I had ever followed. He was growing me in so many dimensions: financial, intellectual, physical, relational, and spiritual. My life's scorecard was being aligned to the Kingdom's culture of multi-dimensional wealth.

Jesus used parables to explain how the Kingdom works and what he expects of us.[83] Some were very short, and yet very powerful. This one really grabbed me:

The kingdom of heaven is like treasure hidden in a field. When a man found it, he hid it again, and then in his joy went and sold all he had and bought that field.[84]

---

[83] Matthew's Gospel has 8 of these parables in Chapter 13. Well worth pondering.
[84] Matthew 13:44, NIV

The serendipitous discovery of the treasure is like the revelation of the Kingdom. It appears suddenly, as it did on my retreat weekend. Kingdom treasure is beyond our wildest dreams.

Like the man in the parable, I immediately knew I had found something extremely valuable. Jesus was irresistible to me. The Holy Spirit filled my heart, and my eyes suddenly saw what was previously hidden.[85] I knew something very good and valuable had captured me. I was full of joy, ready to buy the field.

Jesus is not promoting shady real estate deals! Jesus is saying that the Kingdom is so valuable, it merits everything we have. It is only logical that all our time, talent, and treasure be invested joyfully to own eternal Kingdom treasure.

The Cross was a horrifying way to die—asphyxiation, massive blood loss, the humiliation of being naked, and every passerby yelling insults. Despite the cost, Jesus did it for joy!

For the joy set before him he endured the cross, scorning its shame.[86]

What joy? The joy of setting us free and defeating every enemy, including death. The joy of our worship and allegiance. Quite reasonably, Jesus wants us to make the same "all in" commitment to him that he made to us!

There are many ways to be "all in" with Jesus.

It's a heart posture that trusts and obeys in response to whatever Jesus might ask. You don't have to quit your job or give all your money to the poor. You don't need a seminary degree. You don't have to go to Africa. Just let Jesus lead you day by day.

Here are some short stories of how my friends live "all in".

---

[85] Luke Tofilon's cover design captures the sudden revelation I experienced.
[86] Hebrews 12:2, NIV

Peter Kubasek works in mergers and acquisitions. He is a prayer warrior who works behind the scenes in dozens of Kingdom initiatives around the world. He relates to many wealthy people and shares the kingdom faithfully where pastors would never have the opportunity. He helps them see the Kingdom and invest in eternal treasure. Peter and Maryam have a flourishing family and their home is an oasis of warmth and hospitality.

Laura is a mother of four young boys. Brandon has his own business and serves on the leadership team of his church. Laura is a skilled nurse who stepped back to focus on her kids. She is gifted in prophecy and healing. She prays for people, and they feel God's presence. She leads a group of women every Wednesday morning in setting goals and learning what it means to serve and lead with excellence at work and at home.

Todd and Beth Guckenberger had a burning desire to serve the orphan. With God, they transformed Back2Back Ministries from a local high school ministry into a global orphan care ministry. They had their own kids and adopted more, raising 10 beautiful children together. Todd focuses on the operations, expanding the ministry to six countries. Beth focuses on writing and speaking. They've given vision and leadership through 25 years of faithful work so far, serving tens of thousands of orphans and engaging thousands on mission trips where many were able to see the Kingdom and begin to follow Jesus.[87]

Steve Cesler completed an outstanding international career at P&G. In retirement, he serves on several non-profit boards. While he worked at P&G in Argentina, he and Judi started a new school. They have mentored many young families. Together

---

[87] See back2back.org

they have a flourishing family of 5 kids and 11 grandkids. They are blessing thousands through the ministries they serve.

Over the past 20 years, while raising two kids, Terri has served as an administrator on her church's staff, a schoolteacher, and a real estate agent. Her husband John served as a teacher and leader at their church, while working as a highly skilled engineer and project manager. Their faith echoes to their neighbors, coworkers, and clients.

My friend John Morelock owns a very successful business. Throughout the last 40 years, he focused on his family and his business. He served on a few ministry boards, but mainly used his financial resources to fund strategic ministry initiatives. His passion has been to encourage single mothers and young women with unwanted pregnancies. He encourages pastors over regular lunches and finds reliable cars for ministry leaders in need. I have been encouraged by John, and dozens of young pastors have been blessed with great used cars. John's personal attention and care reflects the humility and grace of Jesus.

Doug's priority is the Kingdom. This is evident in how he loves his wife Sarah and his four young kids. Every Tuesday, Doug opens his house to host a group of young dads looking to be better fathers, husbands, and servant leaders. Some of these dads are exploring the Kingdom for the first time. Doug is a dentist with multiple offices and many younger dentists serving in his expanding practice. He is developing a sustainable way to serve lower-income patients who are in desperate need of quality oral health care. Sarah leads her church's women's ministry, hosts a book club, and is a trusted confidante to many.

Jim and Vivienne Bechtold enjoyed successful international careers with P&G. They helped start a local church that grew exponentially. Vivienne started a ministry reaching out to women in need. Jim leads a bible study for business executives seeking to apply Kingdom principles to their work and serves as the VP of innovation for the CEO Forum. [88]

Luke and Anna have five kids. Anna has a beautiful voice and is a gifted songwriter. Luke works remotely as a designer in the tech space from their sprawling farm and plays guitar and bass. Together with her father, their band plays all over the region. They share their story and sing songs of the Kingdom in between their pop selections. They have a loyal following and often minister personally to their fans.[89]

I met Dan Cathy at a gathering of Christian leaders, where he got down on his knees and shined everyone's shoes. I was blown away that this servant was soon to become the CEO of Chick-Fil-A, succeeding his father who founded the company. Despite their spectacular business success, the Cathy family has an ethic of humble service and Kingdom purpose that permeates everything they do.[90]

These are just some stories of ordinary people living "all in" for the Kingdom. They are successful executives, entrepreneurs, teachers, and parents who have made the Kingdom the focus of their everyday lives.

They are just like the ordinary people in the Bible who lived lives of Kingdom faith, blessing those around them.

Why would these people make the Kingdom their focus?

---

[88] See theceoforum.org
[89] See annaandthedeeperwell.com
[90] See chick-fil-a.com/about/who-we-are

Simple. The Kingdom economy calls us to take our earthly resources and convert them into eternal treasure. It's like the currency exchange that you make when visiting another country.

Take Ecuador for example. Currency instability and rampant inflation led many Ecuadorians to use the U.S. Dollar instead of the Sucre, mainly to avoid constant devaluation. Those who did this early on, for example in 1995, were able to convert their currency at a rate of 2500 Sucre to the Dollar.

These people benefited greatly when the country finally announced it would convert all use of Sucre to the U.S. Dollar on January 1, 2000. The Sucre had devalued to 25,000 Sucre per U.S. Dollar in that five-year window.

Our lives are limited to 70, 80, 90 years. If we believe that this is all there is, we will seek the greatest blessing possible right now. However, if we believe Jesus and live for his Kingdom, we will be thinking about life after death and how to invite as many as possible into a joyful eternity. The outcome of their allegiance to Jesus will be wealth that not only grows now but lasts into eternity through the lives of others.

Knowing that the great devaluation of death is coming, isn't it only logical to go "all in" to maximize our Kingdom wealth? Our time, our talent, and our treasure can be invested to produce the highest possible returns in lasting Kingdom currency. Isn't it sensible to exchange assets from the temporary to the eternal?

We can't take it with us! Our earthly possessions will be of zero value when we stand before Jesus. But the things we have done by faith will be converted into eternal currency. Like the savvy Ecuadoreans, the wise among us will convert as much currency as soon as possible!

So far in this book, I have challenged us to base our lives on the worthiest ideas. I've asked you to think about the Good Life and to live for the life that is so good, it's worth dying for. I've invited you to confront life's brutal realities, and to see the signposts of the better way. I've outlined God's Kingdom vision.

Only the Kingdom gives us the most important things in life, and these things are given by grace, free of charge. They are only accessible by faith. The King and his Kingdom provide fulfillment in the big five areas of human flourishing I mentioned earlier: identity, meaning, purpose, security, and destiny. Let's see how.

Identity is a loaded word these days. We are being placed into identity groups according to our gender, race, socioeconomics, and political preferences. Many battle it out on social media using these distinctions. Groups of all kinds lay identity markers on us, including employers, alma maters, and professional sports teams. We cultivate our identity through our worldview, citizenship, work, affiliations, friendships, possessions, and choices. These are curated with varying degrees of care in our homes, offices, cars, clothing, and social media.

My identity was anchored in my academic and work achievements. My childhood was so stressful and uncertain that I did not have much vision beyond finding stability and comfort. As I started my own family, we focused our goals on kids, work, finances, home, and health. I had no spiritual life despite going to church. When P&G moved us internationally, it reinforced the work identity, provided wildly beyond all our financial goals, and enabled us to build a stable home and family life. But work was the center of who I was.

The Kingdom flipped the script on my identity. I am now the adopted son of a fabulous Father. I am part of a global family. My citizenship is in eternity. I am being freed from a life of self-centeredness. My failures are forgiven. I am no longer guilty, enslaved, or condemned. I have a friendship with Jesus that is not dependent on my performance. It is anchored in his.

Jesus has healed my pain and addictions by switching my pleasure sources to himself. He lifts my head and spreads his protection over me. I am a temple of the Holy Spirit. I do not have to curate my identity or impress others. My identity is in the triune God who is well pleased with me. I am more the "real me" than ever, living the life that I was created to live.

Meaning can be found in many sources. The categories of meaning go back to our earlier discussions about the good life. In a review of 79 studies on meaning in life, researcher Joel Vos proposed five main sources of meaning: physical and material well-being, personal growth and learning, positive relationships and belonging, making contributions to the greater community, and pursuing transcendence or spirituality.[91]

My meaning was derived from achievement, mainly at work. I focused on things like sales and profit growth, innovation, my performance rating, and compensation. Secondarily, I was very intentional about the people I was leading, training, and promoting into bigger jobs. I loved my family but put work first. I had no community and was not pursuing transcendence. That's why my near-death experience rocked me so badly. I had undervalued my health, family, and relationships outside work, and ignored the bigger questions of life.

---

[91] See *Meaning in Life*, Dr Joel Vos, 2018 Edition

The Kingdom changed me from an orphan into an adopted son. My orphan mentality was trying to get a bigger share of a scarce pie. As an adopted son, I was now part of a family with expanding resources and a generous growth mindset. I saw that my greatest meaning would come from my relationship with God. I was loved so much that he died for me. He also gave me the honor of representing his Kingdom.

Is there any greater meaning than helping others find eternal life?

Purpose speaks to the central "why" of our life. Purpose will ideally be found at the intersection of our deepest passions, our highest skills, and the needs around us. This is not limited to your job. It may be a combination of career, vocation, and hobby. Purpose is where you can be happiest, do the best for others, and earn enough to provide for your family.

My purpose was to provide inspiring and curious leadership in building superior brands that would best satisfy the needs of the consumers we served, creating financial returns that would reward everyone. I discovered that I was a strong natural leader when I was 12. My cabin won the Olympics at summer camp because I decided that my best two runners should run on the difficult hill in the middle of the final relay race, not the downhill glory spots at the finish.

I loved to see things that others did not.

The Kingdom reframed my concept of purpose. I was still excited to innovate and build brands that did a superior job of satisfying our consumers. I was still a curious and inspiring leader, and I helped others to grow. But I did not have to be in the limelight anymore; Jesus had decisively taken that spot. I learned that life was not about what I accomplished but how I lived. My fruit was growing on other people's trees.

In my shift to a staff position at P&G, my role was to keep our marketing standards high, to coach the marketing leaders on how to become more effective, and to help develop our next generation of general managers. This involved building trust, coaching, encouraging and challenging. This is how Jesus changed the world with just twelve men. I introduced people to the Kingdom as the opportunities presented themselves and helped them do the same. I was learning my Kingdom purpose: make disciple-makers.

Security speaks to the stability and integrity of our existence. Do we know who we are, and are we confident in our ability to reach our goals? Are we satisfied with our attachments to our parents, partner, kids, extended family, friends, coworkers, and community? Can we say no to others freely? Are we able to meet the demands and needs of daily life? Are we who we appear to be, and are we comfortable in our own skin? Are we free from fear and anxiety?

With the scarcity I experienced early on, I was constantly figuring out where my resources would come from. I was always scoping out the angles. My work brought financial resources beyond my expectations, but I was insecure. The problem with a performance mentality is that it always prompts the question, "What have you done lately?" I was always anxious; life was like a rat race at times. Worry amplifies when you are self-reliant.

In contrast, life in the Kingdom brought deep security. Jesus will never leave me, and he will never be unseated from his position of supremacy. That is lasting security.

Jesus has promised that I will have all I need if I seek first his Kingdom and his righteousness.[92]

That's a huge promise.

Read it again and let it sink in.

This was made practical when I faced high-risk open-heart surgery to fix a birth defect that caused two strokes. I was calm and slept well the night before. I wrote letters to Marianne and the kids and had peace that if this was my time, Jesus would care for them. I did not fear death because I had so much to look forward to. This is still true today. That is ultimate security.

Destiny is the outcome of our lives relative to our hopes and dreams. It is a bigger idea than legacy, which is very important, but only focuses on what we leave behind to others.

Destiny includes the idea of destination and reflects a summation of all these five areas. Have we made our life count? Have we done our best with what we had to work with? Have we invested in others? Have we loved well?

I did not think much about destiny. I did not think about retiring early or sipping margaritas on a beach. I was focused on the future, but more as a survival strategy. I did not have a clear picture of my future other than nebulous things like becoming a CEO, achieving fame, being remembered as a success.

I did not ponder being a grandfather or think about my kids' destiny other than teaching them to succeed so they would not experience the hardships I had.

Jesus got me thinking long term.

---

[92] See Matthew 6:33

Destiny in the Kingdom is a very well-defined choice:

1. Anyone that believes in the Good News of what Jesus did and follows him as King is ushered into his family and his eternal inheritance. As noted in chapter 7, the Kingdom fulfills everything. Jesus calls it heaven.

2. Those who reject the Good News of Jesus will get what they want—a destiny without God, surrounded by others wanting the same. Jesus calls it hell.

With all this in mind, Jesus is totally logical to ask for everything, especially with what it cost him to redeem us. Like the man in the hidden treasure parable, if we have truly grasped the Kingdom, we will joyfully exchange the currency of this world for the currency of the Kingdom!

Marianne and learned this from the example of Bill and Vonette Bright, the founders of Campus Crusade for Christ (now Cru), a global ministry to college students. We had the privilege of spending an afternoon with the Brights in late 2001. They told us about drawing up a contract in 1951 and signing everything over to Jesus. That was powerful.

They had a successful chocolate business, a growing family, and lots of assets. They signed it all over to Jesus unconditionally. God has used Cru to bring millions into the Kingdom. The Brights lived comfortably, but they owned nothing. They lived as stewards knowing everything belonged to Jesus. They were filled with joy having swapped everything for eternal currency.

Later in 2001, we joyfully signed everything over to Jesus. Since then, he has provided for all our needs, as promised. We are no longer owners, we are managers.

Treating Jesus as our true King means transferring ownership of everything to him. It means organizing your life around the King and his Kingdom. Buying that field means putting all your time, talent, and treasure at the King's disposal! It's all his anyway, and he will give you the greatest joy and freedom imaginable.

There are many ways to be "all in" and to buy that field.

Some have no wealth, like Mother Teresa. Some have wealth but use it for the kingdom like David Green (Hobby Lobby and Museum of the Bible) or Dan Cathy (Chick-Fil-A). Some are athletes like Hall of Famer Anthony Munoz (Cincinnati Bengals). Some are scientists like Francis Collins (Human Genome Project) and philosophers like Dallas Willard (USC). Some are Presidents, like Jimmy Carter or George W. Bush.

Following Jesus means going "all in". He will lead each of us by his Spirit in a unique journey. Being "all in" brings a settled clarity and a sense of being fully alive that nothing else can match. King David called that mindset an "undivided" heart.[93]

Being "all in" keeps us steady when life's storms come.

---

[93] See Psalm 86:11

Reflection question:

What things are most difficult for you to sign over to Jesus?

Practical application:

Choose a Kingdom-oriented nonprofit and make a significant investment. As you "buy" Kingdom treasure, notice how the things of this world lose their grip on you.

This "all in" mindset will prove decisive when we encounter the temptations and distractions of the kingdom of this world. That kingdom is opposed to the Kingdom of Jesus. Let's look at the battle between these kingdoms.

Chapter 12

Battle: A Conflict Within.

"There is no neutral ground in the universe.
Every square inch, every split second is claimed by God,
and counterclaimed by Satan."

~ C.S. Lewis

"The greatest spiritual battle of our generation
is being fought between our ears."

~ Jennie Allen

A battle is raging for you, and within you. Have you felt it?

We have an enemy who also has a kingdom. His objective is to destroy us. The first defense against this enemy is to be "all in", with an undivided heart. The second is to learn how to fight the spiritual battle raging in and around us.

But first, let's understand the roots of this cosmic conflict.

We live in a kingdom that is very different from God's Kingdom. The two kingdoms are at odds. Jesus refers to the kingdom of the world as the global system that is opposed to the Kingdom of Jesus and his followers. Jesus calls its leader the prince of this world.

Who is Jesus referring to?

What I am about to tell you may seem utterly fictional. But be assured, this is basic Bible truth acknowledged by theologians throughout the last 2,000 years. Remember the tempter who issued the three temptations to Jesus in the desert? He is the prince of this world. His origin is explained in several different texts of the Bible, which I encourage you to read.[94]

Here is the executive summary. He was among millions of angelic beings that God created first. There are many types of angels— cherubim, seraphim, and archangels, for example. They surround God and give him continual worship. The word *angel* means *messenger*. Angels are often sent to speak to people on God's behalf. The book of Job tells us that the angels were shouting for joy when God created the universe. So, the spiritual realm was created first, and the angels were the witnesses of the physical creation.

They were blown away.

The prophets critiqued earthly kings bent on being gods by telling the story of one of these angelic beings—one who was leading worship in heaven—who decided he wanted to be God. His envy and jealousy erupted into a rebellion among the angelic beings. One-third of the angels went with this rebellious leader, and they were cast out of the presence of God.

These demonic beings are now engaged in a battle in the spirit realm against the good angels and us humans. They seek to destroy human beings as part of their vengeance against God.

Bad angels have the capability to masquerade as good angels, to deceive us. Those who are "all in" will know their Bible, be filled with the Spirit, and be much less likely to be deceived and chewed up by demonic lies.

Because of his actions, the first fallen angel is known as "the Satan", which is the Hebrew word for adversary. Satan used his masquerading skills to enter the garden of Eden as a talking

---

[94] Read Genesis 3, Job 38:7, Isaiah 14:13-14, Ezekiel 28:13-16, Revelation 12:4, John 10:10, 2 Corinthians 11:15, Colossians 2:13-15, Romans 8:19-22, Ephesians 6:10-18

serpent. After casting doubt on the character and goodness of God, he promised Eve that she would be like God if she ate the fruit from the tree of the knowledge of good and evil.

The crazy thing was that Eve was already like God! She and Adam were the only beings made in God's image. Adam passively went along, watching Eve get snookered.

They fell for the same lie that the fallen angel did—the lie of wanting to be God. All humans are the same; we prefer to decide for ourselves what is good and what is evil.

Their decision to trust Satan instead of obeying God's only command was so catastrophic it is known as the fall of man. It is the tragic subject of Milton's *Paradise Lost*. Adam and Eve had taken the authority God gave them to rule the creation and handed it all over to Satan.

Because of this, Satan was installed as the prince of this world. Adam and Eve were sent out of the garden of Eden by God so they would not eat from the Tree of Life. This would have meant eternity in their fallen state.

God clothed them with garments of skin (the first animal sacrifice) and promised that a human descendant would one day return to destroy the serpent.

Jesus was that promised human descendant, and he defeated Satan in the most unexpected way.

He allowed himself to be killed. Satan manipulated the Romans, and sadly, the Jewish religious elite. They were both corrupt, killing Jesus because his Kingdom threatened their status, authority, and wealth.

Jesus outwitted Satan by voluntarily dying on the Cross.

Satan's violent hatred played right into God's plan for Jesus to die in our place. In death, Jesus triumphed over Satan and made a public spectacle of him. [95]

Jesus' sacrificial death covered all human sin, and his sinless lifestyle fully satisfied God's demand for perfect obedience. Jesus won back what Adam and Eve gave away.

Three days later, Jesus rose from the grave, defeating Satan's last weapon, which is death. The resurrection of Jesus was the beginning of the new creation. Jesus provides the same pathway for all who trust him to enter his Kingdom.

We are all born into the kingdom of the world. We remain citizens of that kingdom until we repent and believe the Good News of Jesus. When we are born again, we begin the final exodus from the dark kingdom into the Kingdom of light.

This ancient spiritual battle explains the brokenness we experience in our world. Our sin, compounded throughout hundreds of generations, has taken a significant toll.

Famine, pestilence, genetic disorders, murder, pollution, bankruptcy, divorce, and wars are all examples of the cumulative effects of human sin.

We are in a cosmic struggle between good and evil. The creation is still beautiful, but obviously marred and groaning.[96] The human experience inevitably leads to aging and death. Very few of us escape this life without loss, pain, struggle, or betrayal.

Knowing this, God has endowed us with capabilities of reason and spiritual discernment. He expects us to be able to know him from what he has made. He has given us a conscience with the ability to

---

[95] See Colossians 2:15
[96] See Romans 8:20-22

know right and wrong. God has also given us the truth of the Bible and the power of the Spirit to know and obey his ways.

When we give our allegiance to Jesus, the Holy Spirit enables our adoption into God's family. We become citizens of heaven and legally transfer the authority over our lives from Satan to Jesus.

So how should we live given this conflict?

That takes growth. At first, living in the Kingdom feels unfamiliar. It takes time to find our footing. We must learn a new culture, mindset, and truths, and then integrate those into daily life. The Bible calls this process sanctification: becoming more like Jesus.

I learned that people are not my enemy. We all begin under the influence of the evil kingdom. I could not see this until I believed Jesus, was born again, and received the Spirit's power. Only then could I understand the war going on around me and in me. From there, it is a process to learn the enemy's strategies, repent of our failures, and gain experience and confidence in doing spiritual warfare in the power of Jesus.

The real enemy is Satan and his underlings, who have a hold on people through deception. This view of reality helps us love people far from God, to be for them, and to seek their freedom in prayer, acts of love, and sharing the Good News.

Jesus spoke to his disciples on the eve of his death and encouraged them to be "in the world, but not of it."[97] By this he meant that we would be living behind enemy lines as aliens, strangers, and pilgrims in a world that hates us because it hated him. That's why the apostle Paul gives training in spiritual warfare to his congregations.[98]

---

[97] See John 17:14
[98] Read Ephesians 6:10-18

We live in the kingdom of the world because it is the only way to help others emigrate. In the world, but not of it, we are no longer captive to its leader and his ways. Instead, we are citizens of heaven. As we learn to love others, we will seek them and invite them into the Kingdom of Jesus. Even if that risks the relationship, his love propels us to help others find freedom.

This emigration must happen regardless of our "religion of birth". No matter our origins, Jesus calls everyone to faith in himself and to spiritual rebirth. Walking with Jesus is radically different than practicing a religion. It's a walk of love, allegiance, and obedience of the heart.

This is why Jesus calls us to buy that field. He wants our allegiance over our families, jobs, friendships, money, social position, privileges, and time. It's not that we don't enjoy or care about these things; we simply turn them over to Jesus to deploy any way he wants.

John Wimber phrased it this way: "I am just change in God's pocket, and he can spend me as he chooses."

What does Kingdom life look like in corporate America? It was a daily process of trial and error, learning to do my job like Jesus:

- asking for guidance throughout the day.

- giving encouragement to my coworkers.

- praying before meetings and before sending emails.

I have been crucified with Christ and I no longer live, but Christ lives in me. The life I now live in the body, I live by faith in the Son of God, who loved me and gave himself for me.[99]

---

[99] Galatians 2:20, NIV

152

One example of Jesus living in me at work was the Marketing Directors College. I worked with a brilliant colleague, Mark Schar, to bring the collective wisdom of our recent business initiatives to all 200 P&G Marketing Directors working around the world. Our goal was to help each Marketing Director learn the key lessons everyone else had learned.

We had case studies of successes and failures, experts sharing the latest research on the most effective advertising, new consumer understanding tools, business simulation games, and senior executives sharing their lessons in leadership. We did eight sessions each year, and the group size of about 25 made for an intimate and catalytic learning environment.

During these sessions, I shared a talk on the leadership genius of Jesus. It flowed naturally from my P&G business experience and my growing Kingdom understanding. I spoke about the humility of Jesus, his strategic brilliance, deep understanding of human nature, and his fearless speaking of truth—qualities that allowed him to achieve the greatest leadership impact in history.

I always mentioned John Smale as an example of this type of leadership. John was one of our most effective CEOs. He was humble and caring with people at all levels, and fierce when discussing business strategy and expectations. He was instrumental as a board member in the General Motors turnaround and served to spearhead a major infrastructure renewal in the City of Cincinnati. He was always available to give perspective and coaching to P&G leaders at all levels.

The Kingdom was coming in my work at P&G. The Marketing Director College initiative allowed me to get to know many leaders and to invest in their growth. Some wonderful long-term relationships came from these sessions.

On a flight home from a session in Caracas, Venezuela, I happened to be seated by Virginie Helias, one of our Marketing Directors, originally from France. She was processing my talk on the leadership of Jesus and asked to know more about my story. My story brought her to tears. Then she shared her own spiritual journey and near-death experience, and how that deepened her walk with Jesus. We were both warriors in the battle.

Virginie brings the Kingdom to her family, her local church, and her daily work. Virginie is now P&G's Chief Sustainability Officer, integrating God's directive to steward the planet and its resources into her corporate role.[100] She has made a huge impact on the business with her talent, leadership, and Kingdom perspective.

The battle is exhilarating—and costly.

I've had the privilege of sharing the Good News of the Kingdom with many leaders at P&G and many friends over the years. Some received it joyfully and experienced stunning transformation. Some rejected it and so offended that it ended our relationship. Some quietly think I'm crazy. At times, my own sinful attitudes, actions, and words get in the way.

It's all part of the battle.

It's hard to love people well and obey Jesus while living in a world where two kingdoms are clashing. But we can do this without fear because we know the enemy is defeated. He has no authority anymore, but he still uses deception to hurt and keep people captive to his ways.

An illustration from my visit to Normandy might help.

The D-Day Invasion on June 6, 1944, proved decisive, and Germany was broken. But the final victory was not settled until

---

[100] See Genesis 1:28

the German surrender on Victory in Europe day (V-E Day) on May 8, 1945. Similarly, Satan was defeated when Jesus invaded the kingdom of darkness on the Cross in AD 30. Death was defeated by the resurrection of Jesus. But the day of final victory, when all evil is crushed, will not take place until Jesus returns.

We live between the D-Day of Good Friday and Easter Sunday and the V-E Day of the Lord, when Jesus comes back. The war is won, but skirmishes and losses continue.

We are still living on wartime footing, but most are blissfully unaware. Life in two kingdoms takes courage and stamina.

Why did God set it up this way? I really don't know. My best guess is because of his grace and patience. I'm sure glad he waited for me! He is allowing billions to be born with the hope that many will repent and obey him. [101]

Our assignment is to help them do that.

My sister Marie experienced this two-kingdom battle, and she fought it valiantly and with grace. In the spring of 2008, she was diagnosed with metastatic breast cancer that had spread to her bones. They gave her two years to live. My son Michael and I traveled to Toronto and spent a long weekend with her.

We shared the Good News of the Kingdom with her again, and this time she was ready. She began walking with Jesus. She opened the Bible Marianne had given her 10 years earlier and began to read, study, and grow. We taught her Jesus' seven steps for spiritual growth outlined in the next chapter and she grew as she obeyed and applied the Bible.

Marie was baptized and filled with the Holy Spirit. She was working at GE and began to share about the hope Jesus was

---

[101] See 2 Peter 3:9

giving her. She was full of joy, life, and optimism. This confused her coworkers given her health diagnosis. She told her story and invited many of them to a small group she started in her home. In the next three years, some of her coworkers and friends came into the Kingdom.

Marie lived three more years and was able to witness the wedding of her only son Matt and the birth of her first grandson Charlie. She went home to her King peacefully, having fought the good fight with joy and courage.

This two kingdoms challenge was described by Augustine in his classic book *The City of God*. Augustine was a leader in the early church in North Africa during the time of the collapse of the Roman Empire. In the book, he says that followers of Jesus live in two cities, which was his metaphor for the two kingdoms. He called them the city of man and the City of God.

The city of man is the world, ruled by the demonic forces, with the Roman Empire being a blatant manifestation. This city is always deteriorating, from worse emperor to worse. Even though it looks strong at times, it doesn't last. The City of God is the eternal Kingdom, ruled in the grace of Jesus.

Even though the two kingdoms are at war, the Father, Son, and Holy Spirit rule over both. Satan is a created being and is no match for God. Both kingdoms will eventually be ruled by the righteousness and justice of God. In the meantime, the goodness of God's Kingdom flows into the messed-up reality of the kingdom of the world. Slowly, silently, one heart at a time. Even in places like Hong Kong and Nuremburg.

We are here for a purpose.

That purpose is to help others discover the Kingdom and to become disciples of Jesus who will make disciples. This is so challenging that it can only be effectively accomplished by those who are "all in" with Jesus. It will involve trials, risks, lost friendships, accusations of insanity and much more.

But we are in good company, right there with Jesus!

It's a real battle. The enemy seeks to steal, kill, and destroy. We fight these evil agents in the name of Jesus and have his power to control our thoughts, lift curses, cast out demons, heal the sick, and conquer death. I'll close this chapter with a story.

Paula is a teacher's aide, and she led troubled Justine to faith in Jesus during a crisis of identity. Justine grew with a genuine faith but was always tormented by mental illness and thoughts of suicide. Despite much love and multiple efforts to help her shake her demons, Justine took her own life.

But even in this horrible darkness, God was at work. Suicide is not an unforgivable sin. God's grace covered Justine in her moment of brokenness and brought her home from the life she could not manage. Justine lost her battle, but her Jesus had won the war. Paul teaches us to fight in God's power:

Finally, be strong in the Lord and in his mighty power. Put on the full armor of God, so that you can take your stand against the devil's schemes. For our struggle is not against flesh and blood, but against the rulers, against the authorities, against the powers of this dark world and against the spiritual forces of evil in the heavenly realms. Therefore put on the full armor of God, so that when the day of evil comes, you may be able to stand your ground, and after you have done everything, to stand.[102]

Jesus has won the war. We stand in battle, by his love and power.

---

[102] Ephesians 6:10-13, NIV - Verses 14-18 give further details for praying in power.

Reflection question:

How is the battle of two kingdoms affecting you and the people you care about?

Practical application:

Put on your spiritual armor and ask God to protect all the people that came to mind in the reflection above.

This spiritual battle raises the stakes and the necessity of following Jesus. And there is a practical secret to winning our battles - let's find out what that is.

Chapter 13

Growth: Seven Steps to Lasting Change.

"We have as much of God as we actually want."

~ A.W. Tozer

"If you love me, keep my commands."

~ Jesus of Nazareth

The Internet was exploding, and companies were rushing to stake out territory in the new digital space. I was focused on finding a competitive advantage online for P&G the way my predecessors had done in radio and television. We hosted a national Summit on the Future of Advertising to gather leaders and attempt to establish principles for online marketing.

Our team of young marketing leaders reached out to invite tech CEOs, venture capitalists, consultants, and academics. I asked one of those leaders, Pete Blackshaw, to mentor me on the Internet and help me understand what this might mean for our business. This was not merely a new medium for marketing; it was bringing tectonic disruptions to our business model.

Despite the threat, there was inertia—our brands kept doing what worked before. The opportunities to target consumers more precisely were offset by the limited reach of the Internet and the limitations of bandwidth and message quality. As Amazon, eBay, and AOL grew, I could see that we were headed for trouble. I encouraged brand experiments and shared relevant case studies with our Marketing Directors. We began to place more bets in the digital space. It was a beginning, though I wondered if it would be enough.

I looked for new ways to do my job the way Jesus would do it. I prayed and asked the Spirit for wisdom in the big changes swirling around me. The Holy Spirit was real to me and giving me great joy in my work. I was sharing my kingdom story with coworkers. God was opening doors.

I was invited to speak at the Mayor's Prayer Breakfast in Cincinnati. I shared the Good News of the Kingdom to a roomful of leaders. Many indicated their desire to follow Jesus, asking for follow-up mentoring. I spoke in another ten cities over the next few years to similar groups. In each place, God used his work in my life to bring others into the Kingdom.

During the busiest and most exciting years of my life, I started taking Seminary classes. I was ravenously curious about the God who had changed my life. He gave me freedom and joy and wowed me with his genius, love, wisdom, and presence. I wanted more.

God was at work to develop me and stir up passion to share the Kingdom Gospel; first to kids, then teens, and eventually to adults. My mentor Bob Buford, author of the book *Half Time*, noted that God often paved a second lane along your life's work, creating a smooth transition when he was ready to call you into your next Kingdom assignment.

As time went on, it became clear that the Lord was shifting my heart from work at P&G to more dedicated Kingdom work. We began considering major changes in our family's finances. I was too young to take early retirement, which meant big questions like health care, college tuition, and lifestyle. Yet the gentle tug of the Lord persisted. He was asking for trust.

One day in the fall of 1999, I was in Hebrews chapter 11, studying the life and faith of Abraham. I felt the Lord say that the time to leave P&G was now. When I went upstairs to tell Marianne, she pulled a plaque out of her desk drawer, entitled "The Road to Ministry." She purchased it the day before. That was crystal-clear confirmation. Later that morning, I told my boss Bob Wehling that I was being called into a Kingdom adventure.

In early 2000, I left P&G. I wrote my organization to explain my decision. Many wrote encouraging notes of support, but most found it baffling. I had one of the best jobs in the company, literally at the pinnacle of the advertising world. The press covered my departure extensively.

The hardest part was that I didn't have a plan for our next steps. That's the antithesis of what P&G people are trained to do! I decided to finish Seminary, share God's Word when I could, and we would trust God with the rest. Like Abraham and Sarah, we obeyed God without knowing where we were going.[103]

Shortly after leaving P&G, we met Dr. Henry Cloud. Marianne had been using his books in small group studies for years. We worked together for three years helping churches build small group ministries aimed at spiritual growth. The time with Henry was a masterclass on how to help people grow spiritually and led naturally into our calling to pastor a local congregation.

Including seminary and the time with Dr. Cloud, the transition from P&G to pastoring a church took four years. Our oldest son Denis decided to go to William and Mary. He met Carrie there, another Cincinnatian who graduated from Mariemont High School on the east side of the city. Her father Harry was visiting campus for lunch, and she invited Denis. When he found out Harry was the pastoral search chair for Mariemont Church, he said, "You need to talk to my Dad."

---

[103] See Hebrews 11:8.

In God's unique way, and on his timing, we were called to lead and serve Mariemont Church. The previous pastor had retired suddenly, and the congregation had been without a pastor for two years. The church had history going back 80 years. Mariemont was a planned community built in the early 1920s and was full of tradition. The community was turning over, and many younger families were moving in. [104]

The congregation's average age was about 55. How would we keep the best of the old and usher in the new things God wanted to do? How could we reach a new generation of families in our community? This felt a bit like the work I had done reviving brands. The big difference was that Jesus had his own playbook on how to renew a church.

With everything we learned from Dr. Cloud, our focus was on the power of small home groups to provide life-changing community that Sunday services couldn't. We hoped to bring lasting spiritual transformation to the congregation in all facets of life—family, work, and community. Jesus doesn't draw barriers between the sacred and secular. It's all his.

Jesus laid out a path of growth through his teaching. And the secret to experiencing the transforming effects of his teaching is obedience. This obedience is not based on willpower, but rather on the power of the Holy Spirit:

Jesus replied, Anyone who loves me will obey my teaching. My Father will love them, and we will come to them and make our home with them.

But the Advocate, the Holy Spirit, whom the Father will send in my name, will teach you all things and will remind you of everything I have said to you.[105]

---

[104] See mariemont.org and mariemontchurch.org
[105] John 14:23 and 26, NIV

What does it look like to pursue growth in the Kingdom?

Jesus used seven key steps with his disciples to produce growth in character, fruit, and multiplication. We've seen these steps in action through the stories in this book. They require effort, wisdom, and perseverance given the spiritual battle we are in.

Jesus taught and modeled seven basic growth steps:

1. *Repent:* Confess, turn from sin, and believe that Jesus set you free into his Kingdom. Repentance must be continuous.

2. *Baptism:* Water immersion to wash away sin, clear the conscience, and experience the resurrection life of Jesus.

3. *Lord's Supper:* As we celebrate communion, we confess, receive forgiveness, and renew relationships with God and his family.

4. *Word and Prayer:* We read the Bible, seek God in the quiet place, hear his voice, obey, and ask for what we need.

5. *Spirit-Walking:* Be filled and refilled with the Spirit daily to embody love for God and others despite the spiritual battle.

6. *Generosity:* Using our treasure, talent, and time to give and serve with Jesus' motive of lavish love.

7. *Mission:* We make disciples of Jesus who will make disciples, repeating generation after generation.

This is Jesus' proven roadmap to lasting transformation.

Beautiful changes took place in my life and in Marianne's as we applied these steps and mentored others. The effect on our family, extended family, and congregation has been so encouraging. As we practiced these seven basic steps together, God helped us grow as multiplying disciples. We were issuing the same Kingdom call we had answered years before.

One of the families in our church left to bring the Kingdom to an unreached people group in Asia. Another business leader who heard my story of obedience is now leading a great church in Mexico. Families that Marianne and I mentored are now serving in leadership in our congregation.

A coworker I mentored twenty-five years ago received a restored marriage and family. In retirement, he mentors men while serving as a part-time minister.

The DNA of the Kingdom is growth through obedience that results in multiplication.

The teaching of Jesus forms a repeating pattern. This is the highly strategic way he operated, by mentoring twelve individuals who would experience his life and repeat the process. These steps include knowledge, experience, and community practice which reinforce one another. This is why the Kingdom has grown to become one of the most powerful forces for blessing in the world.

Fifteen years ago, we made our first trip to Nigeria where our mission partner was translating the Bible for one tribe's language. This area is dotted with villages of families engaged in subsistence farming. We met a local disciple maker named Samuel who was sharing the good news of the Kingdom in their language for the first time. We became lifelong partners.

Over the next fifteen years, Samuel's team saw the Kingdom expand dramatically with 12,000 new followers of Jesus in over 350 small congregations meeting together in villages. These disciples dug wells, taught literacy classes, shared Scripture in their language on solar-powered audio players, helped staff their villages' medical clinics, and shared updated farming techniques that improved crop yields. These villages were flourishing!

One of the five regional chiefs (all of which were Muslims) had forbidden the Christians from sharing the Kingdom message in his villages. However, when the other chiefs told him about the changes in well-being their people were experiencing, the resistant chief changed his mind. Since then, the same community transformation has followed in the fifth chief's villages, with 2,000 new disciples and 50 new congregations loving their neighbors.

At a more granular level, how do you measure Kingdom growth in an individual's life? This is more art than science, but you can tell when Jesus is really the King by a few markers.

First, there is more love in their life. This is what I experienced with Marianne. Love is contagious and noticeable.

Second, obedience to the Scriptures is visible, not by talk but by action. They make new and counter-cultural choices.

Third, humility emerges in their demeanor and speech—it is less about them and more about others. They repent and forgive.

For example, Jeff was loud, confident, and often sarcastic. When he started following Jesus, he asked more questions, listened more carefully, and became aware of his effect on others. He still had the same confidence, but it was a totally different interpersonal experience for his wife, kids, coworkers, and neighbors.

Sometimes the change is physically visible.

Several years ago, a hard-charging professional and her family were new to a nearby neighborhood and started attending our worship services. One Sunday, I felt like God wanted me to interrupt the final worship song and say that someone was wrestling with the idea of surrendering their life to Jesus and today was the day. It was an uncomfortable moment, but I simply obeyed and shared that message. It was crickets for a couple of minutes, then slowly, the sound of Alice's high heels clicked as she walked forward.

The band finished the song while I talked to Alice. Her first question was "How did you know?" I explained that the Father whispered to me. She shared her story and said she had been fighting God, but today was the day. We prayed, and at the end of the song, I introduced our new sister to the church. The next Sunday she was baptized. She looked 10 years younger. Her furrowed brow was gone, and tensely pursed lips were replaced with a broad beautiful smile.

Alice has faced several challenges since, including a painful divorce and work realities that produced severe doubts about her faith. It's part of the spiritual battle we are in. I've seen this "up and down" spiritual journey in many situations, usually related to doubts and disobedience. Sometimes a dark night of the soul takes us off-track. Some go through a deconstruction of their faith. The way back is always repentance and resumption of obedience. There are no short-cuts, and growth often comes in unexpected spurts.

However, fruit will always be produced in the character of a follower of Jesus, even if in fits and starts. This fruit is produced by the Holy Spirit organically—the person's character qualities are strengthened supernaturally. Lack of fruit means that Jesus is not fully in charge of that area of our lives.

I could become irritable when I was interrupted during sermon preparation, especially if Sunday's message was not coming together. My sin was the idol of looking awesome on Sunday. When the idol of appearances was threatened, I displayed very bad fruit.

This is life in the spiritual battle.

I gradually learned to crucify my idols and trust God for the message he wanted spoken. I learned to relax and welcome interruptions without biting people's heads off. When deaths, funerals, hospital visits, and urgent requests put me way behind, I was amazed how God gave me a great Sunday message, sometimes in just a few minutes.

As I learn to trust him with my schedule, I am escaping the slavery of appearances, ambition, and appetites. I'm learning to nail these temptations to the cross:

Those who belong to Christ Jesus have nailed the passions and desires of their sinful nature to his cross and crucified them there. Since we are living by the Spirit, let us follow the Spirit's leading in every part of our lives.[106]

The process of spiritual growth requires grace and truth over time. At times, we need God's grace, and at times we need truth to reshape our thinking. We all need repetition. Growth is not a checklist, nor is it linear.

Brian was a veteran who had experienced horrible trauma in the military. It affected his marriage, parenting, and work. Over a period of several years of listening prayer, he was able to feel loved and accepted, and he began to live in healthier ways.

He was courageous. His wife was so loving and incredibly patient. He worked through depression, anxiety, and trauma. He is still experiencing challenges, but he has come such a long way. God is faithful. Brian and all those around him are being transformed. There are no shortcuts to character growth.

Jesus calls us to abide in him to produce more fruit in our lives. He uses a grapevine to illustrate the principle that we (the branches) need connection to Jesus (the vine) to produce fruit

---

[106] Galatians 5:24-25, NLT

(the grapes).[107] If we are connected, the sap of the Kingdom runs through us, and good fruit is produced. Jesus takes the unfruitful parts of our lives (the unfruitful branches) and cuts them off, so the sap goes to the fruitful branches. He even prunes the good branches, so they can make even more fruit. This can be painful, like it was when he pruned my selfish ambition.

God fuels our growth by giving us spiritual gifts. Spiritual gifts are special abilities given to us by God for blessing others with his love. These gifts include hospitality, teaching and preaching, leadership, evangelism, healing, prophecy, shepherding, wisdom, knowledge, giving, serving, dream interpretation, administration, and encouragement.

These gifts allow a community of believers to bless one another and demonstrate the Kingdom to non-believers. But they can also be a source of pride and divisiveness. Like anything else, the gifts must be used in humility and for the benefit of others in the way of the Spirit. When these gifts are used properly, we can spark tremendous growth and invite many into the Kingdom.

Here are three examples.

1. Tanya was struggling with anxiety. For five long years she did not sleep well and spent her waking hours fretting over all kinds of things. One night at our midweek gathering, Tanya came as the guest of Joanne, one of our regulars.

During the worship time, the Lord gave me direction to invite those dealing with anxiety to stand and receive healing. I invited those affected to stand and prayed for healing. About 4-5 people stood to receive prayer for healing. I saw no dramatic response in the moment.

---

[107] See John 15.

A few days later, Joanne called me to say Tanya had slept well for the first time in five years. A few weeks later, Tanya returned and shared that she had been anxiety-free since that night. Now she and her family are part of our congregation.

Her husband connected with one of our leaders and is now growing dynamically as a part of our fellowship. The gifts of prophecy, healing, shepherding, and wisdom combined with this family's obedience to produce significant spiritual growth.

2. One of our staff members felt God had spoken to him during his morning shower. God wanted our staff to invite families to share the benefits of taking a Sabbath rest every week. We developed a menu of format and content options we felt would be a good starting point and proceeded to invite families.

Over the next several months, we had Friday night dinners for about 100 people. These dinners included celebrating communion, reading the Bible, and sharing ideas on how families with young kids could start building a rhythm of celebration and rest.

Gifts of prophecy, teaching and hospitality were used to encourage dozens of families to slow down, remember what Jesus had done for them, and find practical ways to rest and recharge as they train their kids in the ways of the Kingdom.

3. Marianne and a few of our moms decided to reach out to the families who send their children to our preschool. They held preschool parent parties, serving coffee and baked goods on our patio near the preschool entrance.

The idea was to connect with parents as they dropped kids off and to encourage them to stay a few minutes for conversation. The kids loved the treats, and parents stayed for 10-15 minutes. We got to know the parents and their families, concerns, and perspectives. Over time, several families engaged with us in the journey of spiritual growth.

Transformation does not always happen on our schedule. I noticed a young professional worshiping with us. I learned he was the general manager of a national dine-in restaurant chain, and new to our area. As time went on, we developed a relationship and he shared that he had left the church because he was gay. But he felt drawn to worship and the Scriptures.

We had several discussions as he processed the tension between his attraction to Jesus and his lifestyle. About 18 months later, he was transferred. In his last email, he said he had never felt more loved. Jesus is always at work, even when we can't see it.

There are no shortcuts in Jesus' steps of growth. So don't be discouraged if you have stumbled along in life and experienced setbacks. As we learn to obey and apply the seven major steps of growth, we grow in knowledge and maturity.

As we learn to Spirit-walk, his character qualities are gradually applied to change our character. His gifts enable us to build one another up in love and power. And that growth always leads to outward expansion of the Kingdom because our changed lives point others to Jesus.

Here's an example of what I mean. In 2006, I was asked to speak at a Catholic Men's conference in Cincinnati called Answer the Call. The conference was held in the 10,000-seat Cintas Center, home of the Xavier University Musketeers basketball team.

I had met the organizers at a Bible study, and they wanted me to share my story with their men. Specifically, they wanted me to tell the men that they aren't going to heaven because they are Catholics; they are going to heaven only if they trust Jesus.

My talk went well, but what I remember most was the talk given by Charlie Duke. I met Charlie in the speaker's room, and we chatted for a while as we waited our turns to speak.

Charlie was the lunar module pilot on Apollo 16, and one of the 12 men who walked on the moon. As a kid, I was a nut for the Apollo missions. I was awe-struck to be with a childhood hero. He spoke in the same calm Texas drawl we heard while breathlessly watching Walter Cronkite's daily news reports.

Charlie came back from that momentous mission and soon experienced a crisis of meaning. Would he ever be able to do anything that important again? Was it all downhill from here?

His marriage to Dotty was teetering, and his kids were estranged. He, more than anyone I had met, had the experiences to fill the eternal hole in his heart. But alas, even global admiration and a promotion to General could not fill Charlie's heart.

His story of surrendering to Jesus was powerful. His marriage was restored, as was his relationship with his children. As he shared his Jesus story, you could hear a pin drop.

The General had met the King. He found lasting meaning, purpose, and security. He and Dotty spoke at couples' retreats, blessing thousands with the joy and hope of the Kingdom as they followed and obeyed Jesus.

That is Kingdom growth. Change and fruitfulness that lasts.

Reflection question:

Where does your life most need obedience?

Practical application:

Which of the seven steps of growth on page 163 would best address that need?

The key to transformation is obedience motivated by love for Jesus. One outcome of an obedient life is generosity, which is also motivated by love for Jesus.

Generosity is the heart of the King and his Kingdom. Love manifested as generosity is the antidote to fear. Let's see how in the next chapter.

Chapter 14

Generosity: The Antidote to Fear.

"You give but little when you give of your possessions.
It is when you give of yourself that you truly give."

~ Kahlil Gibran

"For it is in giving that we receive."

~ Francis of Assisi

The Kingdom overflows with abundance. This originates in God's love and power. In love, he generously made the earth and filled it with good things. He did this so Adam and Eve would thrive, multiply, and rule over his creation. And when things went south, he did not hesitate to give his one and only Son for our redemption. Jesus gave everything for us from a motive of generous love.

He gave his Holy Spirit so that we can live the overflowing powerful life Jesus promised us. The economy of the Kingdom is centered on freely giving and receiving. Our King is generous; it's a central signpost of the Kingdom.

Jesus told the apostle Paul that "It is more blessed to give than to receive."[108] Jesus knew that the conflict between the kingdom of the world and the Kingdom of God would make money a battlefield. He wants his Kingdom to be our top priority:

Do not set your heart on what you will eat or drink; do not worry about it.
For the pagan world runs after all such things, and your Father knows that
you need them. But seek his kingdom, and these things will be given to you
as well. Do not be afraid, little flock, for your Father has been pleased to

---

[108] Acts 20:35

give you the kingdom. Sell your possessions and give to the poor. Provide purses for yourselves that will not wear out, a treasure in heaven that will never fail, where no thief comes near, and no moth destroys. For where your treasure is, there your heart will be also.[109]

Jesus gives two radical commands here, and two radical promises. If we give priority to seeking his Kingdom, he promises we will have all we need. Not all we want, but all we need. He is promising a life free from worry if we stay focused on the Kingdom. He is saying if we are faithfully generous, we will store up indestructible treasure in heaven. This is the currency exchange of being "all in" that I outlined in Chapter 11.

Coming out of a background of poverty, this was challenging for me. I was used to helping my family members in need, and I gave to my university occasionally. But I was not generous. I was still infected with a scarcity mentality, always worried I would one day be poor again.

When I came into the Kingdom, I realized that Jesus was generous to the extent of death. The Old Testament frequently mentions the *tithe*, which means a tenth. This was expressed in terms of crops, animals. In our day, this means ten percent of gross income. But this was only a starting point for Jesus! He wanted access to all I had and wanted me to be generous.

Initially it was hard to think about parting with that kind of money. I vividly remember writing my first tithe check. It was scary. But something shifted when I obeyed Jesus' teaching. I experienced a surprising joy and freedom. Since then, we have had all we needed, and miraculously, I haven't worried about money. As our giving continued to grow, scarcity evaporated.

---

[109] Luke 12:29-34, NIV

Generosity set me free from fear.

God also taught us to receive generosity. When Marianne had her first bout with breast cancer, our church family brought meals. One night, a lady from church pulled up to deliver our meal. I had seen her before but didn't know her. She was very shy. She drove an old car. She was neatly dressed but her clothes were far from new.

She had made us a wonderful casserole with bread and salad and a dessert. It was nicely packaged in disposable containers and was obviously made with great love. She brought it in, and we prayed together before she left.

I was bawling my eyes out as the kids followed her out the door. We had so much more than her, but she was wealthy in generosity. Our kids came back in and asked why I was crying. I explained that out of the little she had she had given so much.

It was so beautiful. They asked if we had to pay her back when mom got better. I said no, this is Kingdom generosity, and today we receive. We'll have plenty of opportunities to give!

Jesus was teaching me and my family.

God speaks frequently to direct our time, talent, and treasure. One night I was driving home after a meeting, and I felt the Spirit prompt me to buy two gallons of milk and bring it to the home of one of our single moms. It felt weird, but it was so specific, I knew it was God.

When Lilly opened the door and saw me, she burst into tears. She had plenty of cereal for her two boys' breakfast, but no milk and no money for groceries for a few days. God was using me to bless her and her boys and to show them how deeply and practically they were loved.

In early 2007, we were led to make a significant gift using appreciated stock. At the same time, I felt the Lord tell me to pay off the rest of the mortgage on our house. This involved cashing in a significant portion of our stock market portfolio, but Marianne and our financial planner, also a believer, felt this was from the Lord. Jesus led us to give generously and eliminate our last debt just before the market drop in 2008.

This generous lifestyle, free from worry and fear, is available to everyone who will trust Jesus and make everything available for his use. There are many ways to do this. Christ-centered stewardship ministries like Crown Ministries and Financial Peace University have helped millions to apply principles like delaying gratification, finishing education, finding work that suits our abilities, waiting for marriage to have kids, living below our means, avoiding debt, and trusting God.

Treasure in heaven is more valuable than earthly treasure. One always grows in value, and the other eventually declines in value. The apostle Paul lived a generous life for the Kingdom. He grew up in a wealthy family and graduated from the best rabbinical school in Jerusalem. He knew what it was like to have it all. He knew what it was like to be hungry and to suffer.

He learned to be content in all circumstances.

When he received a gift from the church in Philippi, he made sure that they knew everything they had belonged to God, who would always meet their needs. He refers to their treasure in heaven as their "account", which really stuck with me.

I know what it is to be in need, and I know what it is to have plenty. I have learned the secret of being content in any and every situation, whether well fed or hungry, whether living in plenty or in want. I can do all this through him who gives me strength. Yet it was good of you to share in my troubles.

Moreover, as you Philippians know, in the early days of your acquaintance with the gospel, when I set out from Macedonia, not one church shared with me in the matter of giving and receiving, except you only; for even when I was in Thessalonica, you sent me aid more than once when I was in need. Not that I desire your gifts; **what I desire is that more be credited to your account.** *I have received full payment and have more than enough. I am amply supplied, now that I have received from Epaphroditus the gifts you sent. They are a fragrant offering, an acceptable sacrifice, pleasing to God. And my God will meet all your needs according to the riches of his glory in Christ Jesus.*[110]

The idea of having an account in heaven reminded me of helping my kids open their first bank accounts. Jesus was teaching me to invest and build my Kingdom account. I coined the term L-1233 account (short for Luke 12:33).

I saw my L-1233 account as vastly more important than my 401K and brokerage accounts, not because it would make God love me more, but because it gave me the joy of becoming more like him and bringing his joy and freedom to others.

Generosity will give you more joy than the next toy.

One Sunday, I placed $10,000 of the church's money in envelopes taped under each seat. They contained $50, $100, or $200. I taught on Jesus' parable of the talents from Matthew 25, where three servants got 1, 2 or 5 bags of gold and were asked to produce a return for the owner.

Jesus uses the parable to teach that we are all responsible to earn a Kingdom return for what we have been given: time, talent, and treasure. As I closed the sermon, I told everyone to reach under their seats and take the envelopes and open them. I challenged

---

[110] Philippians 4:12-19, NIV - Bold emphasis mine.

everyone to invest God's money any way they want, using their time, talent, and treasure, to earn a Kingdom return. In six weeks, we would meet and share stories.

Everyone took handling God's money very seriously.

One man added $1,000 of his own money and recruited fellow business owners to do the same, to fund a $35,000 surgery for a father that had lost his job. Others gave the money and their time, inviting friends to join them in giving and serving at a soup kitchen. Others paid for the coffees or groceries of those in line behind them and invited them to pay it forward. The $10,000 snowballed into almost $75,000.

Talk about a buzz. Generosity is fun!

Jesus is calling us to experience the thrill and joy of generously handling all he's given us. As Marianne and I learned to give, we wanted to simplify our lifestyle. We downsized homes and moved seven miles south into Mariemont, a walkable community. That allowed us to shift to one car, and we enjoyed a much more active lifestyle, walking 30-40 miles a week.

With a simpler lifestyle, we were able to increase our giving. We made investments in several local and international ministries, intentionally reducing our net worth over a period of several years to a level that would provide for a basic retirement. We were really encouraged by a book called *God and Money* by two Harvard MBA's who reached similar conclusions about a generous lifestyle.[111]

The joy of generosity infused our lives. We held small group retreats on generosity.[112] We shared stories. Five congregants needing cars were given used cars anonymously. Others invested

---

[111] *God and Money: How we discovered true riches at Harvard Business School* by Baumer and Cortines.
[112] See generousgiving.org Watch videos of amazing generosity stories, and check out their Journey of Generosity.

in three young families committed to kingdom ministry by giving them a house down payment. Some helped families get out of debt. Others began tithing and experiencing God's generosity.

Many found personal freedom and elimination of fear and anxiety as they learned to trust Jesus with money. Some received unexpected raises and bonuses. Over the course of the last five years, our congregation's annual giving increased by 50%, while our numbers grew by 20%. As the spirit of generosity grew, our own kids became generous givers and involved others.

Mariel served at an orphanage and raised $12,000 for a new bus. Patrick watches his nieces and nephews and shares his house with coworkers needing accommodation. Michael and Sammy lived on half their income and gave away the other half over a period of six months to build their generosity muscle. Denis and Robynne housed a Ukrainian refugee family of six for three weeks while they waited for longer-term housing.

Generosity begets generosity.

As the grip of stuff lessens, freedom grows.

Generosity includes our time and our talents. I find generosity with my time to be more challenging than with money. After I meet the demands of work, family, fitness, vacations, and rest, there isn't a lot to spare. This is where simplification and elimination of hurry is crucial. The Spirit helps us determine what is truly God's priority.

Just like eliminating debt will help us be able to be more generous, eliminating hurry by dropping unfruitful priorities will allow us to be more generous with our time and more present with people.

Many of our church's businesspeople make themselves available to counsel widows, single moms, and young families. Their experience in business, law, and finance brings untold wisdom and relief to those needing help. The hours of mentoring, coaching, and sharing meals are a beautiful reflection of the generosity of Jesus.

The promises of God to the generous are astounding. He authored the principle of sowing and reaping. The sparing Sower will reap little. The generous Sower will reap abundantly. God is the inventor of the virtuous circle; he enables generosity to continue by replenishing our resources.

One man in our congregation has stayed in touch with his ex-wife. Led by the Spirit, he sends her money regularly even though not required legally. They have forgiven each other and grown to like each other. She is now considering the Kingdom—an impossible thought for most of her life!

Whoever sows sparingly will also reap sparingly, and whoever sows generously will also reap generously. Each of you should give what you have decided in your heart to give, not reluctantly or under compulsion, for God loves a cheerful giver. And God is able to bless you abundantly, so that in all things at all times, having all that you need, you will abound in every good work. [113]

Generosity spurs creativity and fun. Some of our families hosted pancake breakfasts for their neighbors. Our youth served free soft drinks or water out front of a grocery store while offering prayer.

Some rake leaves or shovel driveways for neighbors. Some have bought groceries for strangers. Some leave a very generous tip for a harried waitress. Some carry seniors' groceries to their car. Many make a meal for someone who just had a baby or a surgery.

There are many ways to share the abundant generosity of our King.

My son Michael worked for a video production company that was contacted by Randy Alcorn's ministry to make a video. They

---

[113] 2 Corinthians 9:6-8, NIV

did not have the budget for a normal video, but Michael loved their message. So, he took it on as a pro-bono project.

He got animation artists and sound techs to give their time and skills. He raised funds and put in $250 of his own money. The 1:30 video is powerful.[114] Michael got an appreciative thank you note from Randy and inside was a $500 gift card.

You can never outgive God.

Our youth went to a local restaurant after their weekly meeting with a plan to activate that day's lesson on generosity by blessing their waitress. The restaurant was packed, and our group of about 20 was seated at two different tables. The two waitresses were swamped and barely keeping up. After a delicious lunch, we pooled our gifts and presented the two waitresses with cash for our $175 bill and a $400 tip. The look on their faces was priceless.

They told other customers about "the crazy church kids". A few minutes later they brought another customer to us who had throat cancer. He asked if we would pray for him. The kids laid hands on him, and we all prayed for him. He was in tears and the restaurant was watching in stunned silence. Two days later he called the office and wanted to be baptized.

I visited his home. Joe repented, confessed his sins, and placed his trust in Christ. He was not very mobile, so I baptized him in his tub using a five-gallon pail of water. Joe passed away a few weeks later. He saw the Kingdom and wanted it. The lavish love and generosity of a bunch of crazy teenagers won his heart.

This Psalm lays out the benefits of a generous life:

---

[114] "Live for the Line," youtu.be/T2A9w2wU1Xw. Randy Alcorn's ministry has really blessed our family. I recommend you start with *The Treasure Principle* and explore all his books on the topics of money, heaven, and eternity.

Praise the Lord. Blessed are those who fear the Lord,
who find great delight in his commands.
Their children will be mighty in the land.
the generation of the upright will be blessed.
Good will come to those who are generous and lend freely,
who conduct their affairs with justice.
Surely the righteous will never be shaken;
they will be remembered forever.
They will have no fear of bad news;
their hearts are steadfast, trusting in the Lord.
Their hearts are secure, they will have no fear;
in the end they will look in triumph on their foes.
They have freely scattered their gifts to the poor,
their righteousness endures forever;
their horn will be lifted high in honor.[115]

Delight in God.

Mighty children.

Generations blessed.

Good outcomes.

Never shaken.

No fear of bad news.

Secure hearts.

Righteousness.

Honor.

---

[115] Psalm 112:1-2, 5-9, NIV

In Jesus, this life is available for people at any income level. Generosity is a mindset. We all have the same time to work with. We all have talents. And we all have some treasure we can share.

It's about cultivating the heart of Jesus.

Generosity is a manifestation of love. Generosity is the antidote to fear, worry and anxiety. Kingdom generosity produces lasting wealth because it converts our earthly resources into eternal treasure that will never lose value.

Reflection question:

How did your Kingdom investment experiment from Chapter 11 affect you?

Practical application:

Make an investment in another Kingdom endeavor. Pray for their work and journal your experience.

So far, I've focused on the "why, who and what" of the Kingdom. I have covered all the basics you will need to lay a good foundation in learning the ways of Jesus.

As we've learned so far, Jesus doesn't promise a smooth ride, but he does promise an adventure of challenge and growth despite the brokenness in and around us.

The rest of the book focuses on the "how" of Kingdom living. The next five chapters are filled with tested ideas that you can use to build a Kingdom lifestyle. They cover almost three decades of experience, so don't try everything at once.

Let the Spirit guide you one step at a time. Listen to Jesus and do what he says, even if it defies your own thinking. (Memorize Proverbs 3:5-6)

Let's start with family.

Chapter 15

Legacy: Blueprint for Healthy Generations.

"The family is the essential cell of human society."

~ Pope John XXIII

"There is no doubt that it is around the family and the home that all the greatest virtues are taught, strengthened and maintained."

~ Winston Churchill

Our family handled my transition from corporate to spiritual leadership surprisingly well. The big questions revolved around costs for school and favorite activities.

Relieved that they could stay in their schools and keep playing hockey and golf, our kids continued to grow in their spiritual journeys. As they finished college and started their careers and families, we all began to appreciate the value of our family ties and the support and wisdom that we could give one another.

In the transition, we faced major challenges together. Marianne had her second bout with breast cancer and underwent multiple surgeries, chemotherapy, and radiation. She handled it with grit and grace, leaning into God's Word and his presence to get through the days of extreme nausea, soreness, hair falling out, and exhaustion.

I had two strokes which mystified doctors until a birth defect was discovered. This eventually required open heart surgery. That was like being hit by a truck and compounded by not having any coaching on how to breathe with the ventilator. I was struggling to get enough air and on the edge of panic when I asked Jesus to breathe for me. His presence filled the room, and he brought me through the crisis.

These challenges affected our family in many ways. They slowed us down, brought us closer, and helped us become much more intentional and appreciative of our relationships. The attitudes we carry during setbacks, along with faith, keeps everything in perspective. Death is no longer something to fear because we have an eternal perspective.

For these and many other reasons, our families are the first and best place to grow a Kingdom lifestyle. Regardless of your family's makeup, we all have great opportunities for Kingdom adventure and influence.

The Bible has wisdom for marriage, parenting, the home, finances, discipline, and everything else needed to build a strong family. The seven steps of growth from chapter 13 are the same steps needed to build an authentic Kingdom family.

Before we dive into family building, let's go back to the roots of family in the biblical story.

After the fall, things got worse. Cain killed his brother Abel. Violence escalated to the point that God flooded the earth and started over with Noah and his family.

That did not go well—Noah got drunk and lay naked in his tent. One of his sons told the other two, embarrassing his dad. Their generations did not spread out over the earth as God commanded. Instead, the people got together and used the new technology of fired bricks to build the Tower of Babel.

Their goal was to reach heaven and make a name for themselves. The desire to be God surfaced again. Our ancestors devised their own way to heaven, and that is still going on - the common fallacy of every man-made religion. God saw their wickedness and introduced multiple languages so people could not cooperate in rebellion anymore. Then people finally scattered over the earth and founded distinct nations.

As the story continued, God used a new way to start over. In the line of Noah's son Shem, God waited nine generations (about 400 years) and selected a man named Abram. Abram was in a pagan family of idol worshipers in Mesopotamia. When the time was finally right, God called Abram, then 75 years old, to leave his family and go to the promised land:

Leave your native country, your relatives, and your father's family, and go to the land that I will show you. I will make you into a great nation. I will bless you and make you famous, and you will be a blessing to others. I will bless those who bless you and curse those who treat you with contempt. All the families on earth will be blessed through you.[116]

Abram believed God and left immediately, beginning a pattern of life-long obedient faith. God changed his name from Abram (exalted father) to Abraham (father of many nations). Abraham fathered Ishmael and Isaac. God chose Isaac to fulfill his promise of blessing every family on earth through Abraham's line.

In the next generation, Isaac had two sons, Esau, and Jacob. God chose Jacob and changed his name to Israel. He had twelve sons, who became the twelve tribes of Israel. They were in captivity in Egypt for 400 years before entering the Promised Land.

In the fullness of time, Jesus was born into Abraham's family line, fulfilling all God's promises to Israel. With Gentiles woven into his lineage, Jesus opened the Kingdom beyond the Jewish people to every family on earth.

---

[116] Genesis 12:1-3, NLT - see Galatians 3:14 for the New Testament affirmation.

Millions of families around the world now walk in faith, following Jesus. These are the multi-national multitudes that God promised Abraham long ago.

Families have served together in all kinds of Kingdom assignments through the centuries. Through faith in Jesus, God made a way to bless every family on earth. That promise includes your family! When you trust Jesus, he will make you into a faithful Kingdom family. It took me a while to grasp that.

While I loved my family, my dad was so trapped in alcoholism that the idea of a family vision seemed out of reach. We simply hoped for a normal week, which was rare. My mother had a child-like faith, loving others in the most difficult circumstances, and she prayed. However, as a family, we did not practice a daily faith life outside of Christmas and Easter and saying grace at meals.

We were not well connected to our extended family. Our grandparents lived two and four hours away, respectively, and we saw them two or three times a year. They were very kind to us, but they did not share lessons in faith, work, relationships, or finances. We missed so many opportunities for wisdom.

We are not an unusual family considering that our Western culture reflects an individualistic Hellenistic worldview. In the West, it's common to move away from our families for college and work, then have kids who in turn do the same. We tend to try to optimize the success of the individual, so we often end up starting over with each generation.

Add to that the common pattern of retiring to some place in the south, and families are most fragmented, arguably when the older generation has the most wisdom to give and the time available to give it.

Transfer of wisdom is not common, consistent, or thorough, and transfer of estate assets is not generally planned and discussed as a family. If there is an inheritance, it is often a secret that is unveiled to the kids when their parents are gone. It can feel like a financial transaction, and it is often separated from the wisdom that produced it.

I am not opposed to moving and seeing kids follow their dreams. We left our families for a great work opportunity that lasted eight years in Asia, and then moved to the States. One son lives in Chicago, five hours away. But we work hard to stay connected to our extended families in Canada and to make sure our kids and grandkids know our family heritage and history.

In the Hebraic culture, the multi-generational example of Abraham, Isaac, and Jacob continues strong. Israeli history and culture place the family before the individual. Most families have a multi-generational story of fierce family loyalty in the struggle for life and survival.

Along with the land, the Scriptures, and the threat of enemies, the Jewish people have a resilient and tightly knit family culture. That legacy was able to withstand the exile, the holocaust, and the threat of being surrounded by their enemies.

They can teach us a lot. Even though Israel is an innovative first world economy, the Jewish identity is still anchored in family, clans, and community. How can we leverage the strengths of the Hebraic culture in the development of our Western families?

One obvious way is to stay connected with our extended families. Another is to band together in small groups with other families to learn from one another and to help one another build our family teams. Remember, God has promised to bless every family who possesses the faith of Abraham!

So how do we build a Kingdom family legacy? Over twenty-five years, with lots of trial and error, we have landed on a blueprint of five key components.[117] I hope these help you get started:

- Vision: A picture of your highest hopes for your family team

- Strategy: The key choices that will fulfill your vision

- Training: The knowledge required to carry out the strategy

- Resourcing: The time, money, and talent required to carry out the strategy

- Rhythms: Common reinforcing habits and activities that foster sustained progress over time

This chapter deals with the first two components of vision and strategy—the why and what of family life. The next chapter deals with the how—practices that will lead to flourishing.

Years ago, we set out to become a family of irresistible influence for Jesus and his Kingdom based on two key directives from Jesus in his Sermon on the Mount. We want to let his light shine through us, so that the people we encounter see the light of Jesus and turn toward our Father in heaven. As we place our primary focus on reflecting the Kingdom and the righteousness of Jesus, we rely on him to give us everything we need to achieve our vision. This makes it his vision, done in his power, on his schedule, for his glory. [118]

Our main mentors in Kingdom family-building are Jerry and Patti Kirk. They have given their lives to the Kingdom, and their "flat out" passion for Jesus has persisted joyfully into their 90s. Their kids, grandkids, and great grandkids, plus spouses, now number over 100 people. They are all following Jesus, and about

---

[117] We are indebted to the work of Jeremy Pryor in his excellent book *Family Revision*.
[118] See Matthew 5:16 and 6:33

60 are engaged in various ministry and missionary assignments. Jerry has pastored three churches and started four non-profits devoted to Kingdom work. He has mentored dozens of pastors and leaders over the years. Jerry's teaching has influenced hundreds of families like ours.

One other family story has influenced us greatly. Ruth is a single woman in her 90s. She never married and is now living in a nursing home. She cared for her ailing mother for three decades while working as a machine operator in a food plant. Her siblings married and had several children to whom she has been a devoted aunt and now great-aunt to their children.

Ruth has had a ministry of prayer and generous giving. I know her prayers for me made a huge difference. Her worn Bible and lists of prayer needs are right by her sitting chair. Her monthly giving was extremely generous. She has been a pillar to her extended family. She has stored up much Kingdom treasure and heaven will cheer loudly when she passes into Jesus' arms.

My point is that no matter the make-up of your family, you can have a huge Kingdom influence. The King can do wonders with anyone who will trust and obey him over a lifetime!

To reach our vision, our strategy is to be a family of disciple makers, in obedience to the final command of Jesus.

Disciple making starts with our kids and grandkids. We believe that even small spiritual beginnings are like acorns. They are destined to become oaks of righteousness because of the power of the Kingdom Gospel and the generosity of Jesus. Like the prophet Isaiah, we see rows and rows of righteous oaks spreading far and wide as we build a family that will honor God for generations and reflect his character.[119]

Our disciple-making strategy has three key choices: the home as a mission base, the church as an amplifying community, and selected partners that help us reach out to our city and the world. Let's look at each individually.

1. Our focus on the home as a mission base is God's design. The metanarrative of the Bible is about the older brother Jesus bringing his lost siblings back into the safe and generous house of the Father. God wants a redeemed humanity living in the Father's house together and ruling over the new creation, as originally intended in Genesis 1. The Father's House is a major theme of Scripture and was referenced by Jesus three times in the Gospel accounts.[120]

Our homes can be like the Father's House: a place of grace and refuge for the hurting, a place of growth for those seeking to be trained, and a place for community to gather and celebrate. This can only happen when the family works together as a team, every member and generation doing its job.

The Scriptures are full of wisdom and practical teaching on the family. That includes the right ordering of relationships, the responsibilities and roles for each sex and generation, training and discipline, resources, and the rhythms of an effective Kingdom family.

Moving into the Kingdom spiritually and moving to Cincinnati physically brought significant changes to our family. We were learning so much about teamwork and what the Bible said about marriage and family. We found a few generous couples who were 10 years ahead of us in the parenting journey and willing to

---

[119] See Isaiah 61:3b-4
[120] See Luke 2:49, John 2:16, John 14:2.

share what they had learned. We got to know their older kids, which made them very credible coaches.

This gave us confidence in setting our own parenting strategies. We learned to confess our sin to our kids so that they learned that Jesus was the Boss and that our house ran on his teaching. We reminded ourselves of the Good News and our adoption into God's family by taking communion together at home. We developed training plans for each child.

We held weekly family meetings to review highs and lows and pray for each other. We also began hosting people in our home—missionaries, exchange students, people needing a place to stay, and young singles seeking growth. We reviewed each person who might live with us with our kids and agreed together on specific expectations.

Opening our home became a great way for us to be on Kingdom mission together while building and strengthening our family. We had some big challenges—one guy we invited to live with us fell back into using drugs in our basement and was crazy enough to leave burned spoons around. But the benefits outweighed the risks considerably.

Home base allows us to be on mission while building our family, avoiding two errors. Some remain insular and family becomes an idol. Others make church their priority and lose their kids.

2. The church is our amplifying community. Every family needs a strong local church to strengthen and amplify its efforts and to provide ideas and support. As we gather with other families to worship and fellowship, we see that the Kingdom is a big, diverse family made up of every possible family configuration. As we hear the Word of God taught and dig into what it means and how to apply it, we are strengthened and challenged. As we connect in our

homes and share our stories, we learn new ideas. We share burdens and support one another.

This is often how mentor partnerships are formed. Our kids connect and learn to socialize in the context of shared faith, and lifelong spiritual friendships can begin to form. As we serve each other using our spiritual gifts, we are edified and encouraged. As we hear of the opportunities to reach our community, city, and world, we are exposed to ministries that may become part of our family's vision. We are made aware of needs, like meals after surgery or childbirth, for comfort in the death of loved ones or divorce, and for fellowship with singles of all ages so that God can place those living alone in families and small groups.

I've mentioned the special bonds formed in our church community. Some of our small groups have met weekly for years, helping one another through life's highs and lows. These small groups endure because members feel known, loved, and valued.

One small group was very special for us because it included our daughter-in-love Sammy's parents Michael and Judy Belanger. It all started when our son Michael and his bride Sammy shared their faith journey as part of their wedding celebration.

Like Michael, Sammy had experienced spiritual transformation in Jesus, and her parents knew it was a miracle. Michael and Judy sought and found a similar Kingdom transformation. Both our families traveled together to Ecuador, and Judy's parents received the Kingdom message. Michael and Judy became small group leaders and have faithfully built into the lives of many others for the past several years.

Growing up watching our small groups meet in our home, each of our kids has found their own life-changing small groups. Denis and Robynne helped many at their church get connected into small groups. Michael and Sammy have led small groups and lately, as they have added eight kids, have connected with two families from our church with lots of kids. They are spending quality time together and sharing insights on parenting, finances, and work. All three families are getting stronger.

3. The third leg of our strategy is to participate with mission partners who serve around the world with the same disciple-making family strategy we follow. Three partner families have enabled us to help bring the Kingdom to the ends of the earth. Dave and Rebecca, David and Carleen, and Fernando and Yadira are treasured examples as we build our family.

Dave grew up in our church before we started serving there. He and Rebecca have given their lives to disciple unreached people groups. They have had a big impact on our family's understanding of disciple-making. They did this by introducing us to strategies that are catalyzing movements of Jesus followers all over the world. Dave and Rebecca have been great examples of authentic, creative, and strategic Christian leaders who always stayed focused on their home and children despite the demands of international ministry.

David and Carleen have given their lives to Bible translation in Nigeria. They published the Dukawa New Testament in 2018. That facilitated the explosion of new disciples and churches I mentioned earlier because the Word of God was finally available in the heart language of the people. They are now working on translating the Bible into additional nearby languages. Despite all the pressures of ministry, they prioritized their family and are giving excellent care to their aging parents. Last year, we celebrated together at their oldest son's wedding. They have built a beautiful Kingdom family legacy, inspiring us to do the same.

Fernando and Yadira have directed a children's home in Mexico for more than two decades. They serve about 50 kids who are orphaned, abandoned, or brought by parents without the resources to care for and feed them. Our family has visited several times, along with dozens from our congregation. It is amazing to see how the experience changes people's perspective. My daughter Mariel served there so many summers that she became fluent in Spanish. Our son Patrick has a love for kids which blossomed at that children's home.

Thanks to the love they received, many of the kids have gone on to college and became teachers, nurses, and missionaries. Most of the present staff are graduates from the home. Many have married and had children, building families that are reversing generational curses and blessing their communities.

Fernando and Yadira did this while building their biological family. Their daughter Fernanda teaches at the home's elementary school, and her husband Antonio maintains the property. They want to succeed her parents. Their son Fernando graduated from dental school and will serve the kids' dental needs as part of his practice.

These friends are not famous, but they are heroes in the Kingdom. They are families on mission, living lives of peace, purpose, and eternal significance.

We want to be like them.

Reflection question:

How could a written family vision and strategy benefit your family?

Practical Assignment:

Find another family to partner with you in developing or updating your family vision.

Next, we will look at three practices that are proven to help families flourish.

Chapter 16

Flourishing Families: Three Key Practices.

"Whoever does God's will is my brother and sister and mother."

~ Jesus of Nazareth

"When trouble comes, it's your family that supports you."

~ Guy Lafleur

Our three key family practices are training, resourcing, and rhythms. We use time-tested biblical ideas practiced by families ahead of us on the journey. Let's look at each in turn.

Training: Our three main training tools are: daily reading and discussion of the Bible, discipleship around the dining table, and learning trips.

1. Spirit-led Bible reading is the key to develop your family's spiritual life. The Bible is the source for knowing God and his purposes for us. Jesus said that his words were full of the Spirit and of life.[121] He promised that his words would never fail to achieve his purposes. Every time we dig into the Bible with prayer and the intention to obey, we get revelation, power, and wisdom.

For adults, this means daily reading, reflection, journaling, and prayer. For kids it means reading the bible out loud at meals or during reading time. We have a variety of kid's bibles.

One of these is so good that I commend it to parents, especially those who are new followers of Jesus. An adult can read the whole thing in a couple of hours. It gives an excellent overview

---

[121] See John 6:63

of the Bible story through selected stories and is beautifully written and illustrated. It is unique in that it links every story to Jesus. Children learn that Jesus was promised multiple times, that he is faithful, and that the whole Bible points to him.[122]

Denis' family reads a Bible passage and devotional every day at breakfast, followed by prayer. Michael's family reads a chapter of the Bible most days at breakfast and dinner. Both families ask their children to share things they remember from the passage, whether it's three words for a three-year-old or a complete paraphrase from the oldest. Patrick is reading through the Bible this year. Mariel does daily Scripture devotions and often journals what God says through beautiful paintings and calligraphy.

Marianne spends one day every week with a grandchild one-on-one—she calls it "Mondays with Mimi". The kids love the individual attention Marianne gives. She plays games, teaches them to cook, goes on hikes, whatever the child wants to do. This features lots of reading including Bible stories. The grandkids swarm her at church asking, "is it my turn tomorrow"?

When the kids begin to read well, I start spending an hour every other week walking through the Bible with them one-on-one. I use pictures of biblical sites and videos to help them enjoy learning more about God and his Word. I call it Papa's Bible College. A key part of this is to train them in spending time alone with God and learning to pray and hear his voice. Oh yes, and there is always a treat. (The rabbi's of Jesus' day used honey on writing tablets to help children associate sweetness with God's Word.)

As grandparents, we want to complement what their parents are doing in learning the Bible and being intimate with Jesus. As I've said earlier, the Bible is by far the best way to do that. When they

---

[122] *The Jesus Storybook Bible: Every Story Whispers His Name* by Sally Lloyd Jones.

reach age 13, we plan to take them to Israel so they can experience God's Word in the people, the land, the history, and the archaeology that testifies to the reliability of the Bible.

2. Next to the Bible, we believe the family dining table is our most powerful training tool. This is where kids are trained to help set, clear, and clean the table with age-appropriate tasks. Here they are trained to sit up straight, listen, and speak as requested. They learn to share their highs, lows, wins, and losses. They learn to be respectful, engaged, and to serve. It is a place of joyful celebration and gentle accountability. Here, we welcome guests. Here every Friday or Saturday, we remember the Sabbath and celebrate the joy of resting from our work.

At these Sabbath meals, we often celebrate communion. At times we go around and give each person a chance to confess one sin from the week. As you can imagine, sometimes this is hilarious. Little Mickey says, "I have no sins." Older sister Tilly says, "Mickey, what about when you pushed Manny down the stairs?" Mickey looks crestfallen and says, "Will you forgive me Manny?" Then hugs all around. So meaningful and beautiful.

I usually break in and say, "Mickey, I've got good news for you!" This leads to questions about what the bread and grape juice represent, and then another thankful cheer for being forgiven by the sacrifice of Jesus. This is a rehearsal of the Good News of the Kingdom. Kids see the adults confessing their sins, and they learn that Jesus is the Boss whose grace means there is always another chance to get it right.

I cannot overstate the power of the table to train and build a multi-generational family. For many families, there are simply not enough meals together at the table in an average week to accomplish much. I urge you to protect your family meals!

Denis and Robynne call their family vision "Open Doors", and their home and table is generous. I love watching their young kids set the table, clear the table, light, and blow out candles, pray, and share Bible stories. Yes, young kids are a challenge because they need constant training and discipline, and they are noisy. But the flip side is that their memories are stupendous, and they grow quickly in knowledge and wisdom.

Kids can be trained to do so much more than we imagine. They trained their boys to walk 10 miles a day three days in a row so they could join us when we walked the Camino de Santiago. Simply amazing considering they were 4 and 6 years old! The capabilities of children are enormous. They are big assets for your family team.

Michael and Sammy's vision is to bring "The Father's Rule" over their home. With eight children, they are in a time of significant training, and they do it with gusto and patience. Their table is alive with conversation, complete with a range of great responses and questions about the Bible reading. Yes, it's loud, but oh so good!

And table training includes having kids contribute. Morning coffee is ground and brewed by Roxy, who mastered the job when she was 5. Tilly cooks two meals a week. Ozzy makes fires for s'mores after meals. The young ones set, and the older ones load the dishwasher and sweep the floor. When things slip a bit, as is normal with kids, they patiently retrain and practice again.

3. The third training tool we use is learning trips. Since 1996, we have taken family trips with an intentional spiritual component. Sometimes it's a mission trip. Sometimes it's just a nice beach for a week with one meal celebrating communion. It has been affected by the ups and downs of teenagers' temporary lack of spiritual zeal (which is normal). I had one-on-one golf trips with

each son, studying Proverbs 1-9. We had grad trips for each child between high school and college, where we reviewed their identity in Jesus and encouraged them to use their unique gifts for the Kingdom. When we took our sabbatical to Israel, we had every member of the family join us so they could benefit from the amazing discoveries we made there. One year, we did a family retreat around the subject of generosity.

Starting in 2010, we began what would become our annual family summit. We gathered for a week focused on having fun together, while taking some of the time to study the Scriptures and specific topics that might help us be more effective as a family. Everyone gives input and leadership from year to year, and we take time to give personal updates and pray over each other. My son Denis had us read *The Power of Habit* and discuss how we could become more disciplined as a family. Sammy brought a teaching she had received on the seasons of life that led to deeper inter-generational understanding.

One year we met over Christmas week and did a family candy cane outreach at the Cincinnati Zoo, with each of us giving five candy canes away with the Good News of Jesus explained from the white, red, and J-shape. Another time, I shared a sobering study of our family history and the toplines from *Triumphs of Experience*. I read *Good to Great* with my three sons, looking for ways to improve at work. Marianne shared a teaching from Dr. Cloud's and Dr. Townsend's book *Boundaries*.

In 2020, we devoted time to discuss racial issues raised by George Floyd's murder and what our response as a Kingdom family could be, including building intentional relationships with people of color to deepen our understanding. One year, we digested a brief history of the church for family application on avoiding common heresies and spiritual pitfalls.

Our weeks away are a real highlight for everyone. We rent a lake house, pontoon boat, jet ski, canoes, and kayaks and enjoy the beauty and great food. We play board games and laugh. We have lots of one-on-one time with each child. Last year, we had our first Cottage Olympics for the kiddos.

I love the opportunities these trips give us to read the Bible with the kids (in between the dozens of storybooks Mimi brings). One morning at breakfast, I was sitting with the seven oldest grandkids, and we read a bible story together. I asked the kids to tell me what they most loved about God.

One said it was the great food he always provides. Another was that he invented cousins. Another talked about the beauty of creation. We went around the table with great answers until we got to Roxy, who was then 6 years old. She said, "What I love most about God is that he's never busy."

That is some serious theological insight for a young girl. That does not happen by accident; it is the fruit of family training. The cumulative effect of these trips has been rewarding. Training is a challenge but bible reading, table life, and special trips make it fun and practical.

Resourcing: Family building requires thoughtful resourcing. That starts with a Kingdom mentality when it comes to the use of our time, talent, and treasure. Our resources are focused on maximizing our Kingdom return as measured by our L-1233 accounts. That means that we build the family team's needs into all our financial plans.

Let's start with treasure, our financial resources. You may be miles ahead of me on this since I did not grow up with any financial training. We started with a gift of their age in dollars every week starting in kindergarten. We expected them to give 10%, save 10%, and only spend 80%. At age 12, we started a monthly allowance of $150 which would be paid for being a fully participating member of the family team. That meant tidy rooms, vacuuming their part of the house, garbage, dishes, and doing their own laundry. This covered giving, saving, and any discretionary purchases.

We introduced them to paid work at age 13 or 14 by having each child in turn be responsible for two acres of lawn care. In this process they learned to manage money and open a bank account. Later, when they could drive, have real part-time jobs, and begin to accumulate more money, we taught them about compound interest and helped them open investment accounts.

We have shared our estate plans with our kids, so they are fully aware of what we intend for them and for the Kingdom. As our kids train their children in these areas, we continue to invest financially, focusing on our grandkids' education.

For time and talent, we trained them on time and priority management, and had requirements for serving at home and at school. Drivers had responsibilities to get younger siblings. They were limited to one sport at a time. We encouraged different talents: music, drama, sports, and leadership. We wanted them to know their identity, talents, and passions as they began to consider university and career options.

To maximize our family resources, we broadened goal-setting a few years ago, moving beyond financial to include relational, physical, intellectual, and spiritual goals, learning to keep the five capitals in balance. We share and pray for each other's goals.

Our kids are learning the same skills of doing great work and keeping good life boundaries. Our son Michael was not thriving in his corporate job. During the pandemic, he learned to frame houses in the late afternoons. He started a framing business in 2022, which gives him great joy, good income, more time for his family, and opportunities to train his kids in the business.

Denis and Robynne have two rental properties that provide passive income. Patrick and Mariel are homeowners and have solid investments with no debt beyond their mortgage. This allows everyone to be generous as opportunities arise.

These are all decisions that have come from listening to God and letting him lead our income and resource management. But not just our own resources, we also leverage the resources available through our spiritual community.

Because we had so many young families in our church, every year I did a family sermon series. They were so impactful because I invited several families to share their application of the Scriptural texts on marriage, parenting, and family life. We benefitted tremendously from the ideas shared.

One family shared their methods of training and discipline. As they taught from the front, their seven kids (aged 18 months to 14 years) sat quietly on stools. The older ones helped distribute notes, and the younger ones sat quietly. A powerful example many of our families put into practice.

Our spiritual community offers each family a wealth of resources. As our kids connected with several older men and women in the church, they asked to be mentored. That included networking for jobs and internships, premarital counseling, use of second homes for vacations or honeymoons, and business advice. Many of these grew into wonderful intergenerational friendships.

I mentioned earlier that Michael and Sammy are close with two other families. Their neighbors, Ross and MaK, share parenting hacks, work out together, and keep each other accountable on finances. Luke and Anna just bought a farm, which is something Michael and Sammy are considering. All three families are thriving because they have authentic community. It is so helpful to build lasting bonds of friendship and encouragement with like-minded Kingdom families.

Several pastors and leaders in our city have also had great impact on our family through mentoring, training, and serving together here or on mission trips. I cannot overemphasize that this kind of community resourcing and generosity is key for a family to become fruitful Kingdom ambassadors.

Rhythms: Training and resourcing efforts need to come together in time allocation and schedules. To be an effective Kingdom family, our third key practice is to build sustainable rhythms that will steadily put us in the presence of God, to hear his voice, and to do what he is doing.

As a father, I have practiced and refined these rhythms and asked my family to join me in some simple daily, weekly, monthly, and annual practices. They work!

1. *Communing:* taking quality time every day to be with the Father, Jesus, and the Holy Spirit. This time includes some or all these things: worship, Bible reading and memorizing, listening, fasting, repenting of sin, getting refilled with his love and his Spirit, asking for what we need, asking for people of peace open to the Kingdom, asking for people to invite into the Kingdom, and for more fishers of men. Start with 30 minutes a day, and you will soon be wanting more time alone with the God who loves you.

2. *Celebrating:* taking an extended time every week to enjoy God and to rest. This time can include some or all these things: worship, assessing the week's lessons, reflecting on what Jesus is doing, asking for eyes to see, asking for ears to hear, examining our spiritual journey, our fruit, our intimacy with God, taking communion together, listening and journaling, and refreshing ourselves as we rest. Set aside a sabbath meal with your family and teach them to rest—non-napping kids can be trained to be quiet for an hour. Take that hour to be alone with Jesus and watch what he does. Then have a dance party, followed by a day of rest and play!

3. *Consecrating:* taking a time monthly to refresh priorities. That can include some or all these things: look at fruitfulness, pray through goals, check attitudes, sharing Jesus in relationships, review our giving, refreshing our vision, fasting, and seeking to embody love in new ways. Try fasting the first day of every month until dinner. Use the morning or lunch hour to check in with God on these subjects, and you will be given peace, purpose, and opportunities for significance.

4. *Conceiving:* taking a time every year to retreat with Jesus. This can include some or all these things: rest, play, soak up beauty, seek God, ask for vision, trying new adventures, and giving thanks. When kids are young and more dependent, do this with your spouse and leave the kids with family or trusted friends. As the kids grow, include them. This can be done in two or three days, but a week is ideal. As you set this time aside, God will fill you with wonderful new avenues of growth, inspiration, and blessing.

Finally, we want a spirit of invitation to simmer through all five of the key ingredients for a Kingdom family. Invitation activates our vision, strategy, training, resourcing, and rhythms. Just as Jesus opened the Kingdom to us, we want our family to do the same for others.

What does this look like?

It is a continual thought process of "Who could be blessed by this?" Use every opportunity to include others in your family's rhythms. We've invited two families to live with us to help them sell their homes before committing to buy their next. One family of 5 stayed with us for 5 months and another family of 6 lived with us for 2 months. These families blessed us, and we learned from each other while enjoying fellowship, fun, sharing burdens, and solving problems.

Who can live with us and help us while learning to manage a household? Families in our church with young children have invited college students to live with them for a year. They get free room and board and are on duty in the house 15 hours a week. The mom gets a break and much needed help, and the student sees what running a house looks like. We sometimes invite teenage friends and extended family members to join our annual summit. They help us get a real break by watching kids for a few hours every day. They get to see a multi-generational family in action while earning money.

Who can come to rake leaves with us? A young man visiting our church heard about raking leaves for elderly neighbors and signed up. He raked eagerly and ended up in a conversation with one of our guys. He shared that he was raking leaves to pay the debt for his drug use and marital unfaithfulness. Several discussions later, he learned that he can't pay the debt, along with the Good News that Jesus already paid it. He joyfully became a follower of the King and "bought that field". It all began with an invitation to rake leaves.

Ivan was divorced and had a young daughter. Some Sundays he was with his daughter, and other Sundays with his girlfriend. He was invited to our men's retreat by one of our guys. They followed up with an invite to their small group. Eventually, he joined our annual discipleship trip to Israel. Along the way, he encountered Jesus, and the Spirit convicted him to restore his relationship with his ex-wife.

Three years later, after repenting to Louise and demonstrating significant character change, Ivan began dating her again. After a year of mentoring in the ways of Kingdom marriage, he proposed, and she agreed to marry him again. This time, they are both anchoring their relationship in Jesus and the ways of the Kingdom. What a celebration! It all began with an invitation.

Don't go it alone - ask someone along.

Who can we invite for dinner? Who needs a place to live for a few months? Who can use this car we are about to trade in? Who in your life needs a glimpse of the Kingdom?

These principles, applied with faith, prayer, and humility, will cause your family to flourish. Try these ideas and use the ones that fit your family. Stay patient, and you will see a great harvest.

I close this chapter by praying this blessing over you:

May the Lord cause you to flourish, both you and your children.[123]

---

[123] Psalm 115:14, NIV

Reflection question:

Which of these practices does your family need the most?

Practical application:

Develop or update the training, resourcing, and rhythm plan for your family. Share it with another family you respect and help each other improve your plans.

With a Kingdom lifestyle flourishing in our home, let's look next at developing a Kingdom lifestyle in your work.

Chapter 17

Work: A Paradigm of Significance.

*"Work becomes worship when you dedicate it to God,
and perform it with an awareness of his presence."*

~ Rick Warren

*"Father, I glorified you on the earth
by finishing the work you gave me to do."*

~ Jesus of Nazareth

My Kingdom journey altered my view of work. Work is mentioned hundreds of times in the Bible, with the first use being God's work in creating the universe. [124] In the first two chapters of Genesis, Adam and Eve are given work to do together as part of the perfect creation. In the last two chapters of Revelation, life in the new heavens and earth will include the work of ruling with God and serving him.

In between, human rebellion and compounded sin has distorted work. We have bank failures, environmental destruction, wage discrimination, Ponzi schemes, harassment, and a host of other problems in the workplace. We see good as well—flashes of honesty, justice, innovation, and blessing. Remember the battle of two kingdoms. As Kingdom people, we are called to a lofty view of work:

Work willingly at whatever you do, as though you were working for the Lord rather than for people.[125]

---

[124] See Genesis 2:2
[125] Colossians 3:23, NLT

Because God ordained all work, all work is due to him. Because he was the first worker, all work is dignified. One of the Hebrew words for worship—*avodah*—also means work. The key to work in the Kingdom is to focus our inner motives so that our work can be an offering for the glory of God. Even the most menial work done with the right motives is sacred.

Remember Jesus washing his disciples' feet?

Some felt that my calling into spiritual leadership was somehow better or more valuable to God. That is simply not true. I have attempted to do what God asked me to do and trusted him with the outcomes. The key point is to obey and give my best. I have many friends who serve God in the marketplace—with careers in business, law, medicine, consulting, and law enforcement.

They are obediently giving their best. That is significance!

Said another way, anyone in the marketplace who works to serve God with all their heart is much more pleasing to him than a priest or a minister who is just going through the motions.

A doctor friend once lamented that he wished he could do more for the Kingdom. He thought he should do more mission trips and serve more at his church. "How many hours do you work?" I asked, and he replied, "About 55-60, depending on emergencies." Then I asked, "How many patients do you see every day?" He said, "About 20-25." So, I said, "You are dealing with important things that could become life and death for 100-125 people every week. That is a big congregation of people! That is your ministry!"

Many of us believe the sacred is better than the secular. But when I pointed out his amazing care for people, his sensitive bedside manner, and his opportunity to pray with willing patients, he was able to see the Kingdom value of his work. For many, the Kingdom turns our occupation into our vocation.

My friends Kerry Bradley and Kerry Olin really helped me understand this idea during our Saturday morning meetings. Bradley worked at Luxottica and eventually became CEO. He prayed for wisdom and effectiveness at work. He prayed for his coworkers. He prayed for the Italian owner and was a witness to him in business ethics, family matters and his failing health.

Olin worked at P&G in HR, and then took a job with Microsoft, where he rose to head talent acquisition. His record of speaking his mind truthfully no matter the cost to himself won the trust of senior executives. These guys helped me see what working for the Lord looks like.

Another friend I mentioned earlier, John Morelock, had a stone with the words "Trust and Obey" installed outside the entrance to his business. It is his daily reminder to dedicate every day to Jesus. His shrewd negotiation skills, his avoidance of debt, and his generous rewarding of his employees has produced a business with loyal customers and buoyant financials. But he always gives the credit to the grace of God.

The quality of my work at P&G shifted as I learned to practice God's presence in the minutiae of the workday. I prayed for wisdom and for my coworkers. The Holy Spirit gave me insight to people that allowed me to coach more effectively. The Spirit gave me guidance on how to spend my time and effort on the highest yield initiatives. I experienced transcendent purpose and significance in offering my work as worship.

The same thing happened in my pastoral work. It can be very draining to walk with people through their problems. Yet they need the best attention and care I can give. The pressure of getting ready for Sundays was constant. Issues with property, our preschool, and our international mission partners were always arising. It is so easy to start shouldering these burdens yourself and ignoring your own. Pastors are burning out and quitting at an alarming rate.

I felt the beginnings of burnout twice. Once when an associate left to start a church nearby. A second time during Covid when a key staff member resigned. Both times, I repented of self-effort and took 10 days away from the church in a beautiful and restful place. I reset my focus on loving and serving God first, and I asked the Holy Spirit for insight.

The Lord led me into repentance and forgiveness. I was able to own my part and bless those involved in the conflicts. I was able to re-engage my work with a healthy disposition. During the weeks that followed, I regained the lightness and joy of serving God and my work was more fruitful than ever.

In the Greater Cincinnati area, many marketplace leaders are bringing the Kingdom in their work in fields like consulting, music, manufacturing, training, and human resources. The following examples illustrate a paradigm of significance in work when we focus on the Kingdom.

Chuck Proudfit was called by God to activate the faith of marketplace people for the sake of the Kingdom. Chuck founded a marketplace ministry called *At Work on Purpose,* a collective of thousands of working Christians in various settings across the Greater Cincinnati Area. Chuck practices what he preaches as a successful consultant and with his indomitable energy, teaches and challenges his community to activate their faith at work. His influence is now expanding as he helps other cities establish Kingdom workplace networks. [126]

Marketplace leaders and pastors formed a collective called City Servants. This group collaborates to connect, unite, and support Kingdom efforts in Greater Cincinnati. One of these leaders is my friend Louis Arnold, who just retired as the police officer responsible for faith community relations. Initiatives to address poverty, policing, prison reform, education, and partnerships have been launched in love by collaborative teams. [127]

Chuck Mingo and Troy Jackson started Undivided, a ministry of racial reconciliation. They started by helping churches, but soon expanded to offer their expertise to companies, non-profits, universities, and civic organizations. They are bringing Kingdom solutions to racism that are changing our city. Undivided is now expanding beyond Cincinnati.[128]

Led by Troy Culbreth, a collaboration of gifted musicians called Cross Worship gathers hundreds regularly to worship Jesus in unity. They are producing high caliber Kingdom music that is speaking to the younger generations, and many outside the Kingdom. Their music has been streamed by millions. Cross Worship has brought unity to our city while sparking artistic expression and creative innovation.[129]

The Greater Cincinnati Prayer Canopy has 50+ organizations with 1000+ people praying for our city. Most of the people praying are marketplace Christians. This effort has literally changed the timbre of our community.

---

[126] See atworkonpurpose.org
[127] See churchesofgreatercincinnati.com/seven
[128] See undivided.us
[129] See crossworshipmusic.com

In December of 2022, we asked people to pray for a spirit of prayer to fill our city. On January 2, 2023, Damar Hamlin, a Buffalo Bills player, dropped dead on the field during the Monday Night Football game here against our Bengals. That event unleashed a torrent of prayer on the field, in the stands, on national networks like ESPN, at the hospital where Damar was being treated, and in workplaces around the city. [130]

The Nehemiah manufacturing company is a partner producer of several of P&G's most important brands. At their facility in downtown Cincinnati, they initiated a Second Chance hiring program for ex-felons and homeless citizens. They have reported that these Second Chance hires have turned out to be some of their most consistent and effective workers.

By offering stable employment and a living wage, Nehemiah has brought hundreds of people back into a productive role in society and helped heal dozens of families. Through their example, dozens of other companies are offering Second Chance jobs to hundreds of people who were previously shut out of meaningful work, housing, and access to the Good Life. This is Kingdom business—redeeming and transforming. [131]

One evening we offered a night of prayer for business owners. Steve had an insurance agency and was seeking prayer for expansion of his business. I asked him if he had signed over the business to Jesus. He said, "What do you mean?" I said, "Jesus already owns it; he's just waiting for you to acknowledge that." He wrestled with the idea that he was a steward. I encouraged him to ask Jesus for the next business expansion idea.

---

[130] See gcprayercanopy.net
[131] See madebynehemiah.com

Sally was looking to start an insurance agency. It turned out that Steve was an agent of the same company Sally was considering. What are the odds of that? Steve was able to pray insightfully and encourage Sally to go forward with a great report on the company's integrity. As we prayed, Sally eagerly dedicated her business to the Lord. Do you see God at work? He knew Steve would give wisdom, and Sally would give faith. Both give customers great value. In the Kingdom, business innovation and collaboration produce blessing for all stakeholders.

Work is the context where transformation can take place for most people. It is where they spend most of their waking hours. Jesus likely took over the family building business when his earthly dad Joseph died, working until he was 30. He knows all about demanding customers and the value of quality work!

We have several Kingdom people involved in financing and supporting new start-ups in our city. Tim Schigel, a successful entrepreneur, founded Refinery Ventures, a purpose-centered venture capital firm. [132] Luke Dooley leads a startup accelerator that also focuses on the well-being of the entrepreneur. [133] Pete Blackshaw leads Cintrifuse, a team dedicated to build the region's tech and entrepreneurial ecosystem.[134] These gifted business leaders exemplify the kingdom paradigm of work:

- a vision for community flourishing

- the sacredness of all work

- the well-being of employees

---

[132] See refinery.com
[133] See oceansprograms.com
[134] See cintrifuse.com

- an orientation to growth and generosity

- love for creativity and excellence

- a commitment to sustainability

- trust in the law of sowing and reaping

This paradigm shifts us from a self-centered perspective of work which produces fear, anxiety, and burnout. By offering our work as worship, and adopting an eternal perspective, we can experience peace, purpose, and significance.

Jesus invites us to make the shift:

Walk with me and work with me—watch how I do it. Learn the unforced rhythms of grace. I won't lay anything heavy or ill-fitting on you. Keep company with me and you'll learn to live freely and lightly." [135]

---

[135] Matthew 11:28-29, MSG

Reflection Question:

What are the strengths and weaknesses of your approach to work?

Practical Application:

How can your work better influence the flourishing of others?

With an integrated Kingdom life at home and at work, let's now look at the challenge of finishing what we have started.

Chapter 18

Finishing Well: Wisdom to Go the Distance.

"It's not how you start, but how you finish."

~ Michael Phelps

"The one who stands firm to the end will be saved."

~ Jesus of Nazareth

Bob Buford (1939-2018) was a successful Texas entrepreneur who built a very profitable cable TV business. In 1984, he sold it and invested his resources to start the Leadership Network, a nonprofit dedicated to help strengthen the impact of nonprofits and churches.

In 1994, Bob published *Half Time*, a book describing his own move from a life of personal success to a life of significance. His book captured the vision and opportunity I felt God had given me. Bob and Linda helped us set our vision for season two.

Bob had a wide impact in the Kingdom, coaching and networking hundreds of people like me through their second career transitions. Bob published *Finishing Well* in 2004, profiling the lives of sixty people who had shifted from their main careers to a second career focused on the Kingdom. Some had been at their second career for a while, and others like me were in the process of making the transition. The rich lessons from these case studies helped me make the most of the last two decades.

But that wasn't Bob's last revelation!

As Bob analyzed the life expectancy and financial resources we enjoy, he saw the opportunity for a third season. He was no longer leading the Leadership Network but found himself primarily mentoring others who were in active day-to-day leadership.

He described this next shift as the move from significance to surrender. This is the move from being the active leader to being a source of wisdom for others. Bob finished strong in 2018. He has his Kingdom reward, including a reunion with his son Ross who had drowned in 1987 at age 25.

This idea of graduating to wisdom work was beautifully modeled by Bob's mentor, Peter Drucker (1909-2005). Dr. Drucker was the premier author, educator, and consultant on management and leadership in the 20th century. His ideas influenced the philosophical and practical foundations of the modern corporation. Along with Bob, Peter saw the nonprofit sector as a crucial ingredient in building a complete society.

Peter wrote two-thirds of his books after the age of 65 and used his wisdom to influence leaders long after he retired. Bob and Peter influenced *Good to Great* author Jim Collins to write the monograph *Good to Great and the Social Sectors*. My successor Jamie Moore and I read it together, and he used it to shape his vision for the church's next season.

At our surprise retirement celebration, the emcee for the evening was a former parishioner, investigative journalist Ben Swann. We were amazed that he brought his entire family from Atlanta. He has a way with words. Ben declared that we were re-firing, not retiring. This captures the way we feel as we consider our next season of Kingdom life. We won't be giving official leadership anymore, but Marianne and I hope to continue investing in others by sharing the wisdom that we have gained.

We have several role models in this regard. Jerry Kirk has continued to connect and pray with his 100+ family members regularly, and with us, well into his 90s. Mike Cambron, Burr Robinson, Tom Dewey, Zeke Swift, and Louis Arnold are in their 70s and early 80s. Long-time leaders in our congregation, they are pouring out wisdom to the next generation of leaders.

My friend Mike Combs sold his business five years ago, but he has not stopped tending to his Kingdom assignment in his late 70s. I always joke that the Devil calls Mike the grim reaper because Mike has led several of his oldest friends to trust in Jesus while on their deathbeds. Mike is currently mentoring four young men in the ways of the Kingdom.

I've often said that I want to be like them when I grow up, and now it is my turn!

One of the best seasons in my career with P&G was working with Vidal Sassoon (1928-2012) when we launched his line of hair care products in Japan. Vidal had sold his salons and product line many years earlier, and P&G had acquired the Sassoon brands with the purchase of Richardson-Vicks. Vidal still received royalties and remained very engaged. The launch in Japan was highly anticipated, following the great success of the Rejoice and Pantene brands a few years earlier. We had very strong consumer feedback, and the marketing team headed up by my lifelong friend Tom Blinn had developed a powerful introductory launch campaign.

We were betting the farm on the launch, and something very special happened. Vidal, then 65, was received like royalty by the Japanese beauty press. Unlike the U.K. and U.S., where he was considered over the hill, Japanese culture respected the aged. Vidal was honored and celebrated as the expert—the sensei of hair and style. The free publicity was worth millions and gave the brand a priceless image endorsement that helped generate record sales and profits. Vidal finished strong, having more impact in his last twenty years than ever.

If you are reading this and you are thirty years old, I am challenging you to think long-term for yourself and your generations. You may start a company or stay in the same line of work throughout your life, but you have opportunities to have a Kingdom impact as you grow and develop your skills, and as you mature. It starts with taking the long view of your career.

A fantastic resource for that is *The Long View* written by my friend Brian Fetherstonhaugh, who recently retired as the Chief Talent Officer of Ogilvy Mather Worldwide. Brian encourages us to start strong, reach high, and go far.[136]

To your success, seek to add significance and surrender. They are not mutually exclusive. Don't live to retire one day; live every day for the Kingdom. If you are older or near the end of your career, it is never too late to start following Jesus and to have a life of eternal impact.

You may not know about George Mallory, but I bet you know about Sir Edmund Hillary. George Mallory led climbs of Mount Everest 30 years before Hillary's successful climb in 1953. It is unknown if Mallory ever reached the summit, although it is certain he was the first to climb above 8,000 meters. His body was found in 1999—sadly, the camera he carried was not found.

---

[136] See thelongviewcareer.com. Brian offers great value, including free downloadable resources to help you analyze your career status and strategize next steps.

So, we don't know if he made it to the summit. What we do know is that he did not make it down. Sir Edmund Hillary summitted and made it down. Charlie Duke walked on the moon and made it back. This is what finishing well looks like in mountaineering, and space travel, and it's the same with life.

What are the barriers to finishing well?

It's all about character.

Looking at Bible characters, many did not finish well. Some, like Abraham, Joshua, Daniel, Mary, Peter, and Paul finished strong. They stayed connected to God, did not let their successes go to their heads, and didn't give up when the going got tough. Others, like David, Hezekiah, Gideon, Eli, Solomon, Samson, and Saul, either finished poorly or failed to finish.

Please study their stories for yourself. They are interesting and revealing narratives, given as examples and warnings for us. What were the key factors in their failures? I found six flaws in their characters that can help us avoid finishing poorly.

1. **Pride:** Usually accompanied by fear and anger, pride has its roots in thinking we know better than others and God. This is why pride is often called the gateway sin. Moses, in fear of a mutiny and in anger with the rebellious people, pounded on the rock and took credit for the water that God caused to pour out. This moment disqualified Moses from entering the promised land. It did not terminate his relationship with God; it just ruined its quality. I spent way too much time thinking I was better than others, going it alone, and putting myself in the place of God. I shudder at the thought.

2. **Love of money:** Many wrongly think money is the root of all evil, but it's not. *It's the love of money.* Judas Iscariot oversaw

the finances of Jesus' ministry. He complained that a woman wasted expensive perfume on Jesus when it could be given to the poor. But he did not care for the poor, and he often used the money for his own purposes. Judas betrayed Jesus for thirty pieces of silver. Growing up in scarcity, I saw money as the way out, as a savior. I certainly loved money.

3. **Sexual immorality:** King Solomon presided over one of the most wealthy and powerful kingdoms ever seen on earth. He had incredible wisdom that kings and queens from all over the world came to hear. Yet he ended up with 700 wives and 300 concubines. He was so distracted by the women in his life that he started worshiping their gods. He finished poorly and missed much of what God had for him. My addiction to sex and pornography consumed my life and almost destroyed my family. It was foolish to worship this false god.

4. **Abuse of power:** At the height of his power, David stayed home from war and idly walked around on the roof of his palace. He saw a woman bathing. He used his power to have her brought to him and essentially raped her. Her husband Uriah was one of his most able and faithful warriors. Despite his loyalty and honor, David arranged for Uriah to be killed in combat. David abused his power to commit adultery and murder. He was restored to God in a powerful time of repentance[137], but his kingdom slid into chaos. I treated a few people at P&G poorly, taking advantage of my position and power. No longer a Lone Ranger, I've avoided that by having accountability in my life, with a team overseeing me at church and three good friends who connect quarterly.

---

[137] See Psalm 51. God forgives as we repent, but we still must face the consequences.

5. **Family breakdown:** David's son Amnon was attracted to his stepsister Tamar. Rather than ask for her hand in marriage, he raped her. David failed to discipline Amnon, likely because his sin drained his moral authority. His brother Absalom plotted Tamar's revenge, and eventually had Amnon killed. Then Absalom plotted to steal the kingdom from his father, creating chaos, division, violence, and death. My infidelity and my absent fatherhood almost destroyed my family's future. Only the truth and grace of Jesus saved us from generational disaster and untold pain.

6. **Complacency:** King Hezekiah had a terminal disease, but cried out to God who healed him and gave him 15 more years of life. During that time, Hezekiah collected riches and proudly showed off his wealth to many visiting dignitaries. Once he had his health back, he put everything on cruise control. God warned Hezekiah that he was going to bring foreign invaders, but not until after he died. Rather than repent, Hezekiah fell into a deadly complacency. Even though complacency is not my pattern, I know that I can never stop depending on God and obeying his prompts.

Aside from avoiding the negative character flaws above, what good habits can help us finish well? Through this book, I've shared six habits that bear repeating in summary form:

1. **Focused purpose:** There is staying power in knowing why you are here. My purpose is to help others meet the King and enjoy Kingdom life. My purpose helps clarify when and where I need to say no, to preserve my energy for the things Jesus has given me to do. This focus has helped the friends I mentioned earlier remain fruitful with age. This is just as the Scriptures promise, if we keep focused on our purpose:

They will still bear fruit in old age, they will stay fresh and green, proclaiming, "The Lord is upright; he is my Rock, and there is no wickedness in him."[138]

For we are God's masterpiece. He has created us anew in Christ Jesus, so we can do the good things he planned for us long ago.[139]

2. **Settled identity:** Knowing who I am is equally important to having a focused purpose. If all I have is my purpose, my satisfaction will go up and down with my results. In knowing that God has secured my identity and my future, I am free to pursue my purpose without the extremes of anxiety when things are not going well, and pride when they are. Because the Father has adopted me into his family based on what Jesus did, I can do nothing to advance my security. I simply receive his approval and serve him gladly. He has already secured my value and destiny.

3. **Solid community:** The friendships I've mentioned in this book have formed the backbone of my community. Leaders without community become isolated and vulnerable. This book has been made better by my friends. The best ideas in my marriage, parenting, mentoring, and ministry have come from the example and lessons learned from my friends. The failures and losses of life have been mourned and processed with these friends. They have rebuked and coached me. Because God himself is a triune community, the Kingdom is a community of giving and receiving. We are not our own; we belong to Jesus and each other.

---

[138] Psalm 92:14-15, NIV
[139] Ephesians 2:10, NIV

4. **Healthy lifestyle:** Because of the fall, we are all experiencing aging and one day we will all experience death. Many factors will determine when that happens, including genetics, accidents, and natural disasters. In the meantime, our bodies are temples of the Holy Spirit. They deserve care in matters of sexual purity, moderation in eating and drinking, and rest. We are called to train our bodies in godliness, to work diligently, to carry out our Kingdom assignments, and not to worry. To do our part in finishing well, we need the healthy lifestyle described in the Bible.

5. **Generous love:** We are called, like Jesus, to give away our lives. Generosity of heart means that our time, talent, and treasure will be given to others in love. Generosity will bless many and it will be multiplied. A generous heart is contagious and gives great honor to those around us. A generous heart gives a winsome picture of the King and his Kingdom. Generosity keeps the great enemies of fear and self-preservation at bay and the abundant life front and center. The generous will be honored by the King.

6. **Humble spirit:** Humility is a quality in ancient literature that was considered a liability until the first century. The God who was not stingy with his privileges humbly became a man and went to his death for us. Jesus altered the desirability of humility. Humility produces life-long learners. Humility acknowledges that spiritually, we are all beginners. The humble will keep seeking spiritual growth, renewal, and vitality, and will stay refreshed, vibrant, and resilient. They will not rest on their laurels. The humble ones keep growing and constantly increase their return on spiritual investment.

The movie *Facing Nolan* illustrates this humble spirit. Nolan Ryan pitched 27 major league seasons. He tallied 5,714 strikeouts, almost 1,000 more than any other pitcher in history.

He pitched a record seven no-hitters, the last one when he was 44 years old. He had another five no-hitters broken up in the 9th inning and holds the record for the most complete game 1-hitters with twelve.

Nolan is finishing well by investing in his family. While he holds 51 major league records and a World Series title, he never won the Cy Young award as the best pitcher in the league. Fellow Hall of Famers are shocked to hear this; they all guess he won three or four. The humble stay focused on what matters. For Nolan it was his team winning.

I am in my mid-60s and can be certain I am on the back nine of life, but I am not certain of what hole I am playing.

In season three, I want to keep serving the King, sharing his Kingdom Good News, and making disciple makers.

I want to finish strong. I'm betting you do too.

Reflection question:

Which of the six barriers feels most applicable to you?

Practical application:

Which of the six key habits feels most important to you?

I hope that your heart has been won over by the costly love of Jesus, and the sheer scope of his Kingdom.

Nothing comes close to knowing God's love!

We have walked together through the practical ways of Jesus in living an enduring Kingdom lifestyle.

I trust the book's title no longer feels like hyperbole.

My earnest hope is that you are well on your way to a life of peace, purpose, and significance.

Only one additional step is needed. Jesus commands us to love others by sharing the Good News.

Let's talk about sharing The Biggest Idea Ever.

Chapter 19

Pay It Forward: Sharing the Big Idea.

"God authorized and commanded me to commission you: Go out and train everyone you meet, far and near, in this way of life, marking them by baptism in the threefold name: Father, Son, and Holy Spirit. Then instruct them in the practice of all I have commanded you. I'll be with you as you do this, day after day after day, right up to the end of the age."

~ Jesus of Nazareth

"And pray for us, too, that God may open a door for our message, so that we may proclaim the mystery of Christ, for which I am in chains. Pray that I may proclaim it clearly, as I should."

~ The Apostle Paul

We can be thankful that God himself is so missional. Where would we be if he just hung out in heaven and left us to our own devices? Thankfully, he gave us his Word and his Life. Jesus came for us and gave it all so we could know him and his Kingdom. The Kingdom is the Good Life!

The love of Jesus compels us to share the Good News. Having experienced that love, we'll be keen to share it with those we love and care for and those we live and work with.

That's exactly what Jesus asks us to do.

But first, let's start with some research into some common spiritual beliefs. [140] A recent study by the Barna Group showed why we need to be sensitive as we share the Kingdom.

---

[140] See barna.com This is US data but likely representative of the English-speaking world.

The following percentages represented those in full agreement with each of the statements below:

24% - "I have heard everything church leaders have to teach."

34% - "The Church does not answer my questions."

36% - "My beliefs aren't aligned with the Christians I know."

51% - "I distance myself from the politics of the Church."

This is a big challenge for every follower of Jesus.

We are far from perfect. The mission of Jesus has gotten mixed up with buildings, money, and politics. Many churches are not connecting meaningfully with unchurched people.

The polarization of the culture has stunted discourse, and discussions of faith are received poorly in the public square. In this context, followers of Jesus are naturally defensive.

The world of the first century was even more hostile to the message of Jesus. Yet, he has left us with a mission – to make disciples that make disciples.

The mission of Jesus was first given to twelve ordinary men that he lived with for 3+ years. He showed them his ways of doing things. When it was time, they went into the world the way he did, moving relationally through their natural networks and finding others who would do the same.

It's a very long story to understand how this missional approach of Jesus was lost, so I won't bore you with the details.

Fortunately, the ways of Jesus and his disciples are being rediscovered today by paying close attention to the stories in the four accounts of Jesus' life (Matthew, Mark, Luke, and John), the book of Acts, and the letters written by his followers. These methods and the necessary lifestyle to make them work are very clearly described in these Scriptures.

Like the seven steps of transformation in Chapter 13, there are also seven steps to inviting others to follow Jesus:

1. *Pray* - people don't come to Jesus unless God draws them. Remember the spiritual battle around us? We must pray!

2. *Train* - teach others to talk about Jesus and to find the people of peace that God has been preparing.

3. *Engage* – serve your community and ask the people of peace to gather their friends to hear and discover God's Word.

4. *Obey* - ask the Spirit to guide leaders and explorers into understanding and obedience.

5. *Coach* - as they grow, coach discovery groups to follow the seven growth steps in chapter 13 as they become a church.

6. *Multiply* - teach church members to repeat steps 1-5 and plant new discovery groups.

7. *Release new leaders* - as new churches are formed, train new leaders and release them, and repeat the process.

In the 300 years after Jesus, the church grew to represent about 10% of the population of the Roman empire, about 6 million Christ-followers. This was done in a world where they were powerless, ridiculed, and marginalized.

They had no buildings, seminaries, or Bibles like we do today. It was all done by ordinary people sharing Jesus stories they had memorized, reading copies of the Apostle's letters, and spreading the Word in their natural networks, meeting in their homes, and loving their neighbors.

Obedient disciples are now catalyzing amazing movements of new believers all over the world. More than 100 million new disciples have resulted from these efforts, and 8 million new churches have been started in the past 30 years. Very few of these churches have buildings, they typically have 15-20 people meeting in homes. [141]

Marianne and I recently returned from a trip to Nairobi, Kenya where we met 250 of these ordinary people who are catalyzing movements in 45 countries.

They are sharing the love and Good News of Jesus and encouraging everyone to do the same. They are demonstrating the power of reading God's Word, obeying what they learn, serving one another in a community of generosity, and inviting friends and neighbors to join in and do the same.

We will tell friends about a new film or restaurant that we love. How much more important is it to share what Jesus has done for us and to invite others to discover the same for themselves? We have more Kingdom opportunities than we can imagine.

Here are two recent examples.

I sent a draft of this book to my friend Michael who lives in Canada. We worked together for several years in the 80's. He is a devout Jew. After reading the manuscript, he had many questions. He was surprised to learn Jesus was Jewish and that he could follow Yeshua (his Jewish name) while continuing to be Jewish.

One day he called me excitedly to share that he was following Jesus. Like the early Jewish believers (Peter, John, and Paul) he had discovered that Jesus was his true Messiah.

We walked the 800 kilometers-long Camino de Santiago in the fall of 2022. We met people, shared stories, and talked about the Kingdom. Robert was from Germany and Bethany was from China, and they were drawn to each other.

Marianne and I had long days walking through Spain, talking about God and sharing stories. They wanted the Kingdom.

---

[141] See Motus Dei, edited by Warrick Farah. See also newgenerations.org

Their engagement led to Zoom calls to study what the Bible says about marriage. It was a privilege to marry them and pray with them as they set out to build a Kingdom family.

All we did was share the love of Jesus and his work in our lives.

So, where do we go from here?

Here are a few ideas for you to consider as you think about sharing the Biggest Idea Ever:

1. Consider inviting a group of friends, extended family, or coworkers to read this book together. Read and discuss 1-2 chapters a week. Share your reflections and applications.

2. Continue the journey by reading and obeying Bible passages together. You don't need experts, only a desire to obey and apply what you learn. Appendix A provides a series of Bible stories you can read and apply together.

3. As you apply Scripture, you will be following the path in chapter 13. You're becoming a church, but don't freak out! Remember my sister Patty's church in a muffler shop? Your house church is now a part of Jesus' Kingdom movement. Just stay focused on loving each other and obeying.

4. Develop leaders. Appendix B provides a list of Kingdom classics that will help deepen you and other leaders who emerge from your group. There are more resources available to help you on my website: www.denisbeausejour.com

5. Encourage your church to invite new people and start new discovery groups like you did in point 1 above. Keep repeating the process, just like the early church!

Each of our stories is unique. God can use anyone willing. My story is just one of many. I'm not special, but Jesus is. He can do miracles through you if you are willing to trust and obey!

Jesus works with ordinary people through the trials and disappointments of life. It won't all be roses. As I have shared in these stories, following Jesus involves suffering, heartbreak, setbacks, and failures.

His Kingdom is an opposed work.

But his promise is to never leave us. He will complete the good work he has begun in us.

Love the Father.

Trust and obey the King.

Walk in the Spirit.

May Jesus and his Kingdom become the heartbeat of your life, so that you, your friends, and family can trade anxiety, fear, and burnout for peace, purpose, and significance.

Appendix A:

Stories to Discover Together

In each week's meeting ask these seven questions:

1. What am I thankful for? Leads to thanksgiving.

2. What challenges do I have? Leads to prayer.

3. Who needs help, or who can we serve? Leads to service.

4. Did I do what I said I would last week? Accountability.

5. What does today's text say? Leads to revelation.

6. How will I apply this text personally? Obedience.

7. Who will I share this with? Leads to multiplication.

Study one story each week in your discovery group:

1. Creation of the world - Genesis 1:1-2:3

2. Creation of the man and woman - Genesis 2:4-25

3. The first sin and judgment - Genesis 3:1-24

4. Sin spreads to the children of Adam and Eve – Genesis 4:1-16

5. Sin spreads to the whole world, God sends the flood – Genesis 6:11-22, 7:11-23, 8:14-22

6. God's promise to Abraham - Genesis 12:1-9, 15:1-6

7. God gives a substitute sacrifice for Isaac - Genesis 22:1-19

8. Abraham's descendants enslaved, God chooses Moses as liberator - Exodus 1:1-14, 3:1-9.

9. The Passover: the blood and the lamb – Exodus 12:1-28

10. God gives His ten laws and sacrifice for breaking the law – Exodus 20:1-21, Leviticus 4:1-4

11. God's people continually sin – Judges 2:10-23

12. God promises a Redeemer – Isaiah 9:1-7, 52:13-53:12

13. Birth of Jesus according to prophecy – Matthew 1:1-25

14. Baptism of Jesus – Matthew 3:13-17; John 1:29-34

15. Temptation of Jesus – Matthew 4:1-11

16. Jesus has authority to forgive sin: The paralyzed man and four friends – Luke 5:17-26

17. Jesus has power over nature – Mark 4:35-41

18. Jesus has authority over spirits – Mark 5:1-20

19. Jesus has power over death – John 11:1-45

20. Jesus has power to give eternal life -- John 4:1-26, 39-42

21. The Last Supper: This is my broken body and blood shed for you – Matthew 26:18-30

22. Jesus is betrayed, arrested, falsely accused, tried, and sentenced to death – John 18:1-19:16 23.

23. The crucifixion, deciding for or against Jesus: It is finished! – John 19:16-42

24. The resurrection and appearance to his disciples and followers – Luke 24:1-35

25. Jesus returns to the Father: The Ascension – Luke 24:36-53

26. Our Response: The New Birth – John 3:1-21, Acts 2:36-41 John 11:25-26

27. Read the book of Acts, then Romans - one chapter per week

Appendix B:
Resources for Growth

Bibles, Study Apps, Devotionals, and Prayer Apps

Study Bibles in the NIV, ESV, and NLT versions

Study Apps: YouVersion, Blue Letter Bible, Bible Hub

My Utmost for His Highest by Oswald Chambers

Knowledge of the Holy by A.W. Tozer

Prayer Apps: Lectio 365, Pray As You Go, Pause

Making Disciples of Jesus who will Make Disciples

Spent Matches by Roy Moran

Contagious Disciple Making by David Watson

Miraculous Movements by Jerry Trousdale

Theology/Answers to Tough Questions

Knowing God by J.I. Packer

Systematic Theology by Wayne Grudem

Heaven by Randy Alcorn

The Divine Conspiracy by Dallas Willard

Is Atheism Dead? by Eric Metaxas

Confronting Christianity - 12 Hard Questions by Rebecca McLaughlin

The Kingdom Unleashed by Jerry Trousdale and Glenn Sunshine

Hearing God's Voice and Experiencing Him

Hearing God by Dallas Willard

Why I Am Still Surprised by the Voice of God by Jack Deere

Experiencing God by Henry Blackaby

Personal Growth

The Road Less Traveled by M. Scott Peck

Changes that Heal, Integrity, and Trust by Henry Cloud

Hiding from Love and People Fuel by John Townsend

Family and Business

The Shaping of a Christian Family by Elisabeth Elliot

Family Revision by Jeremy Pryor

Every Good Endeavor by Timothy Keller

Anointed for Business by Ed Silvoso

Israel - God's Faithfulness on Display

Miracle of Israel by Gary Frazier and Jim Fletcher

Start-Up Nation by Dan Senor and Saul Singer

Reclaiming Israel's History by David Brog

Acknowledgements

This book was written in the past year, but it was birthed over the past four decades, with lots of help.

My wife Marianne has been my best friend for 43 years. I owe much of my spiritual growth to her constant prayers for me. She is a fierce and courageous bride, an amazing mother to our four children and a loving, patient, doting, and fun Mimi to our ten beautiful grandchildren.

She has patiently read and given valuable feedback to this book, and happily encouraged me as I wrote and edited. This book is deeply shaped by her love, grace, and insightful feedback.

Two of those decades were spent in executive leadership with an innovative global company, where we lived and worked in 5 countries and served or consulted with dozens more. I am so thankful to my colleagues at P&G who were gifted, humble, and fun to work with.

The other two decades were spent serving as the leader of a vibrant spiritual community, Mariemont Church. Many of those folks are marketplace leaders in the fields of business, law, medicine, teaching, and engineering. We learned much from each other and from our partners serving all over the world.

I am thankful to each person mentioned in this book. Their stories have changed and transformed me. I have omitted some last names and changed some names to protect their privacy.

My family has influenced this book in profound ways, and I want to thank each one by name.

My son Denis and daughter-in-love Robynne and their kids Den and Julien. My son Michael and daughter-in-love Samantha and their kids Tilly, Ozzy, Roxy, Manny, Mickey, Clarity, Red, and

Duke. My son Patrick, the amazing uncle. My only girl Mariel, and my son-in-love Wade Curtis. Our beloved Pappy, Michael Combs. And Nacho the energetic Vizsla.

Jerry and Patti Kirk inspired us to build a multi-generational Kingdom family and demonstrated faithfulness in prayer and service to others. They exemplify the love of Jesus.

I am indebted to Dr. Henry Cloud and Dr. John Townsend whose writing, teaching, and personal examples have deeply shaped us and our family.

Thanks to my early readers who provided crucial feedback. I am especially grateful to my friend Elizabeth Miller Wood whose brilliant edits to my query letter inspired me to improve my craft. Look out for Elizabeth's debut novel, she is a fantastic writer.

My friend Beth Guckenberger gave me so much good advice.

John Pepper has been a lifelong example of leadership integrity and a valuable mentor to me and to so many. John gave me insightful comments on the manuscript and much-needed encouragement through his own books. His coaching during my tough patch in Australia and his wisdom in pushing me to go for a girl will never be forgotten by me or my family.

My sister Michelle Forsyth and her husband Cam supplied warm hospitality and a perfect place in their cool comfortable basement for me to write without distraction. They love us and our entire extended family so well. I am confident great things lie ahead for them in a very challenging season.

In all things, one Friend has brought everything together for my good and for his fame. He is the only Way to receive every benefit in this book. He is the real Author of this work, and He and his Kingdom will forever be The Biggest Idea Ever. This work is dedicated to Jesus, my great King.

About the Author

Denis was born in Campbellton, New Brunswick, Canada, and spent his early years in Ottawa. He graduated from Michael Power High School in Toronto, and from the Queen's University Smith School of Business in Kingston.

He worked at Procter & Gamble for 22 years with executive assignments in Toronto, Sydney, Kobe, Hong Kong, and Cincinnati. His last assignment was as VP of Advertising.

Following a call into spiritual leadership, he completed seminary at Trinity Evangelical Divinity School in Chicago, then led Answers for Life, the ministry of Dr. Henry Cloud with Campus Crusade for Christ (now called Cru).

Following that, Denis and Marianne were called to lead and serve Mariemont Church, a very special spiritual family.

In retirement, Denis and Marianne continue as spiritual mentors. Denis serves on the boards of New Generations and the Greater Cincinnati Prayer Canopy.

Denis and Marianne love building our multi-generational family together. We seek to reflect the Kingdom, honor the King, and encourage others to experience The Biggest Idea Ever, which includes these amazing promises for all our generations:

They will be called oaks of righteousness, a planting of the Lord for the display of his splendor.

They will rebuild the ancient ruins and restore the places long devastated; they will renew the ruined cities that have been devastated for generations.[142]

---

[142] Isaiah 61:3b-4, NIV